M000169459

THE LITTLE BOOK

of

INVESTING

LIKE THE

PROS

Little Book Series

In the *Little Book* series, the brightest icons in the financial world write on topics that range from tried-and-true investment strategies to tomorrow's new trends. Each book offers a unique perspective on investing, allowing the reader to pick and choose from the very best in investment advice today.

Books in the *Little Book* series include:

The Little Book of Investing Like the Pros by Pearl and Rosenbaum
The Little Book That Still Beats the Market by Joel Greenblatt
The Little Book That Saves Your Assets by David M. Darst
The Little Book That Builds Wealth by Pat Dorsey
The Little Book That Makes You Rich by Louis Navellier
The Little Book of Common Sense Investing by John C. Bogle
The Little Book of Value Investing by Christopher Browne
The Little Book of Big Dividends by Charles B. Carlson
The Little Book of Main Street Money by Jonathan Clements
The Little Book of Trading by Michael W. Covel
The Little Book of Valuation by Aswath Damodaran
The Little Book of Economics by Greg Ip
The Little Book of Sideways Markets by Vitaliy N. Katsenelson
The Little Book of Big Profits from Small Stocks by Hilary Kramer
The Little Book of Currency Trading by Kathy Lien
The Little Book of Bull's Eye Investing by John Mauldin
The Little Book of Emerging Markets by Mark Mobius
The Little Book of Behavioral Investing by James Montier
The Little Book of Hedge Funds by Anthony Scaramucci
The Little Book of Bull Moves by Peter D. Schiff
The Little Book of Alternative Investments by Stein and DeMuth
The Little Book of Bulletproof Investing by Ben Stein and Phil DeMuth
The Little Book of Commodity Investing by John R. Stephenson
The Little Book of the Shrinking Dollar by Addison Wiggin
The Little Book of Stock Market Profits by Mitch Zacks
The Little Book of Safe Money by Jason Zweig

THE LITTLE BOOK

of

INVESTING

LIKE THE

PROS

5 Steps for Picking Stocks

JOSHUA PEARL
JOSHUA ROSENBAUM

FOREWORD BY HOWARD MARKS

Contents

About the Authors

Please feel free to contact JOSHUA PEARL and JOSHUA ROSENBAUM with any questions, comments, or suggestions for future editions at:

josh@investinglikethepros.com

JOSHUA PEARL, AUTHOR

JOSHUA PEARL has served as a Managing Director at Brahman Capital, a long/short equity asset manager. He focuses on public equity investments and special situations utilizing a fundamentals-based approach. Previously, he structured high yield financings, leveraged buyouts, and restructurings as a Director at UBS Investment Bank. Prior to UBS, he worked at Moelis & Company and Deutsche Bank. He received his BS in Business from Indiana University's Kelley School of Business. He is also the co-author of *Investment Banking: Valuation, LBOs, M&A, and IPOs.*

JOSHUA ROSENBAUM, AUTHOR

JOSHUA ROSENBAUM is a Managing Director and Head of the Industrials & Diversified Services Group at RBC Capital Markets. He originates, structures, and advises on M&A, corporate finance, and capital markets transactions. Previously, he worked at UBS Investment Bank and the International Finance Corporation, the direct investment division of the World Bank. He received his AB from Harvard and his MBA with Baker Scholar honors from Harvard Business School. He is also the co-author of *Investment Banking: Valuation, LBOs, M&A, and IPOs.*

RAYMOND AZIZI, EDITOR

RAYMOND AZIZI is a Portfolio Manager at Weiss Multi-Strategy Advisers where he manages a long/short equity portfolio. Previously, he was an investment professional at Lehman Brothers Merchant Banking where he focused on leveraged buyouts and growth capital investments. Prior to his private equity role, he worked in the Investment Banking Division at Lehman Brothers. He received his BS in Business from Rutgers University and his MBA from The Wharton School of the University of Pennsylvania. He is also a contributor to *Investment Banking: Valuation, LBOs, M&A, and IPOs.*

JOSEPH GASPARRO, EDITOR

JOSEPH GASPARRO is a Vice President in Capital Services at Credit Suisse where he advises on capital raising and operations for alternative asset managers. Previously, he executed M&A and capital markets transactions in the firm's Investment Banking Division. Prior to Credit Suisse, he worked at BofA Securities and UBS. He received his BA from Gettysburg College and his MBA from Rutgers Business School. He is a two-time recipient of the President of the United States' Volunteer Service Award. He is also an editor of *Investment Banking: Valuation, LBOs, M&A, and IPOs.*

Foreword

~

Howard Marks
Co-Chairman and Co-Founder, Oaktree Capital Management

In 2011, I wrote a book called *The Most Important Thing: Uncommon Sense for the Thoughtful Investor*. I intended the title to be somewhat ironic, since in investing there is no single most important thing. A huge number of elements have to be taken into account in every investment decision, and the process has to be broad and yet detailed, both methodical and creative.

How can would-be investors or those on the way up learn about all of these elements and how to incorporate them into their methodology? *The Little Book of Investing Like the Pros* by Joshua Pearl and Joshua Rosenbaum is a terrific source of help in this regard. It will quickly get the would-be stock market investor started up the learning curve.

Simply put, I have never before seen a book that provides the same complete and thoughtful orientation to the process of investing. *The Little Book* is clear, logical and well-organized, a concise survey course in what investors need to know. It starts at the beginning, with identifying candidates for investment and screening them for potential. Then it progresses to studying the subject companies' finances as well as gauging the potential of their businesses. It moves on to the essential element of gauging whether the attributes that have been identified are highly valued at the stock's price or a bargain. And it concludes with thoughts on how to determine the role the stock can play in an investor's portfolio. It illustrates these lessons by way of the example of companies that are followed throughout the book.

The bottom line for me is that *The Little Book of Investing Like the Pros* provides a simple introduction to a far-from-simple field. Superior performance in the competitive field of investing requires both covering the nuts-and-bolts elements that most experienced investors are familiar with, and mastery of nuanced considerations that will lead to success only if the investor understands them better than others.

Identifying and learning to grapple with the former will free the reader to turn to a meditation on the latter. I'm glad *The Little Book of Investing Like the Pros* is at hand to accelerate the reader's progress. It does an excellent job of introducing the decisions that have to be made. You'll find learning to make them well to be a fascinating lifetime's work.

Acknowledgments

~

We are deeply indebted to the numerous colleagues, peers, and friends who provided guidance, input, and hard work to help make this book possible.

Special thanks to **Mitch Kuflik** and **Rob Sobel**, co-founders of Brahman Capital. Following my [JP] many years in investment banking, they gave me a shot to be a professional investor. After providing a gateway into the investing world, they helped me expand my skill set and offered sage advice over many years. Their decades of experience and wisdom have been invaluable in my career development. My family and I are forever indebted to them.

Two of my [JP] mentors **Jeff Schachter** and **Mitch Julis**, who also happen to be close friends with each other, were incredible influences on this book. It simply could not have been completed without their support and encouragement along the way. Personally, I've tried to emulate these two individuals and mirror the way they think, act, and live their lives. They are both "mensches" in every sense of the word.

Our vision for this book could not have been realized without the help of **Raymond Azizi** from Weiss Multi-Strategy Advisers, whose investing insights, experience, and primary research were priceless. Ray is among the most talented portfolio managers we know and is a third co-author in every sense of the title. Most importantly, he's one of our closest friends. **Joseph Gasparro** of Credit Suisse was critical in the editorial and production process, including streamlining and refining the ultimate work product. Joe has a vast network, unyielding can-do approach, and an innate ability to get things done. He has been a true partner to us for many years.

We would like to highlight the important contributions made by **Brian Johnson** of Barclays and **Dan Levy** of Credit Suisse, both highly regarded equity research analysts. Their contributions were multi-dimensional and their unwavering enthusiasm, insights, and support were nothing short of exemplary.

Special thanks to Delphi Automotive's retired CEO **Rodney O'Neal** and retired Chairman **Jack Krol** for serving as the inspiration for our case study and helping to guide the narrative along the way. Aptiv CEO **Kevin Clark**, Chairman **Rajiv Gupta**, Board member **Sean Mahoney**, and **Elena Rosman** of investor relations shepherded our book internally, provided sage feedback, and helped ensure the details were accurate.

Didric Cederholm provided deep insight on the Delphi bankruptcy process and facilitated access to many of the key players involved. The Silver Point Capital team, consisting of co-founder **Ed Mulé** and **Jeff Forlizzi**, provided perspective on the full Delphi backstory, including the labor-intensive process towards creating massive shareholder value.

Jeremy Weisstub provided sound technical insights and helped us distill complex concepts into layman's terms. **Milwood Hobbs, Jr.,** a mentor and colleague dating back to early investment banking days, provided constructive feedback and was critical in getting the right people on board with the book. He still serves as a valuable friend and partner over fifteen years later.

We'd like to thank the outstanding team at Wiley, who have been our partners for over a decade on all of our books and courses. **Bill Falloon,** our acquisition editor, brought us into the Wiley family and never wavered in his vision and support. He has provided strong leadership over the years and has become a true friend.

Our publisher **Matt Holt** championed our book both internally and externally. **Michael Henton, Steven Kyritz, Michael Freeland, Susan Cerra,** and **Purvi Patel** on the editorial and production side worked diligently to ensure all the details were addressed and facilitated a smooth production process. **Jean-Karl Martin,** our marketing manager, helped us realize our vision through his creativity and foresight.

We also want to express immeasurable gratitude to our families and friends. **Masha, Jonathan,** and **Olivia,** and **Margo** and **Alex,** thank you so much for your support, patience, and sacrifice. You were always in our hearts and minds as we worked diligently to produce a book that would make us all proud.

This book could not have been completed without the efforts of the following individuals:

Raymond Azizi, *Weiss Multi-Strategy Advisers*
Nadav Besner, *Sound Point Capital*
Didric Cederholm, *Lion Point Capital*
Maimi Chow, *Time Warner, Inc.*
Christopher Clark, *Soros Capital Management*
Kevin Clark, *Aptiv PLC*
Juan Pablo Del Valle Perochena, *Orbia Advance*
Michael Evelson, *Kingdon Capital Management*
Bryan Fingeroot, *Raymond James*
Jeff Forlizzi, *Silver Point Capital*
Joseph Gasparro, *Credit Suisse*
Joshua Glassman, *Goldman Sachs*
Greg Gliner, *Ironwall Capital Management*
Michael Goody, *Scharf Investments*
Steven Gordon, *J. Goldman & Co.*
Michael Groner, *Millennium Partners*
Rajiv Gupta, *Aptiv PLC*
Tim Hani, *Bloomberg*
Han He, *Oaktree Capital Management*

Milwood Hobbs, Jr., *Oaktree Capital Management*

Benjamin Hochberg, *Lee Equity Partners*

Cal Hunter, *Barnes & Noble*

Robert Jermain, *SearchOne Advisors*

Brian Johnson, *Barclays*

Mitchell Julis, *Canyon Partners*

Jennifer Klein, *Sequence Capital*

Jack Krol, *Delphi Automotive*

Shaya Lesches, *Young Jewish Professionals*

Marshall Levine, *GMT Capital*

Dan Levy, *Credit Suisse*

Jonathon Luft, *Eagle Capital Partners*

Peter Lupoff, *Tiburon Family Office*

Sean Mahoney, *Private Investor, Aptiv PLC*

David Marino, *BGC | MINT Equities*

Dave Miller, *Elliott Management*

Edward Mulé, *Silver Point Capital*

Rajeev Narang, *Hudson Bay Capital*

Justin Nelson, *J.P. Morgan*

Rodney O'Neal, *Delphi Automotive*

Daniel Reichgott, *Federal Reserve Bank of New York*

Eric Ritter, *Needham & Company*

Elena Rosman, *Aptiv PLC*

Jeff Schachter, *Crawford Lake Capital*

Howard A. Scott, *Park Hill Group*

Hooper Stevens, *Sirius XM*

Anne Tarbell, *Trian Fund Management*

Jeremy Weisstub, *Aryeh Capital Management*

Disclaimer

❧

Views Expressed All views expressed herein are those of the Authors as of the date of publication and do not represent the views of their respective current or former employers, or any entity with which the Authors ever have been, are now, or will be affiliated. The information and views expressed herein are subject to change at any time without notice. The Authors and John Wiley & Sons, Inc. (the "Publisher") are not under any obligation to update or correct any information provided in this book.

Informational Only; No Investment Advice The information provided herein is for general informational purposes only and is not and should not be regarded as "investment advice," a "recommendation" of any kind (whether investment, financial, accounting, tax, or legal), or "marketing material" of any kind. This book does not provide recommendations or views as to whether a stock or investment approach is suited to the financial needs of a specific individual. Your needs, goals, and circumstances are unique and may require the individualized attention of a licensed financial advisor.

References and Examples Illustrative Only Any and all examples included herein are for illustrative purposes only, and do not constitute recommendations of any kind, and are not intended to be reflective of results you can expect to achieve. Any reference to any company in this book is not intended to refer to, nor should it be considered, an endorsement of any stock, brand, or product.

Information Accuracy   Although the information provided herein is obtained or compiled from sources believed to be reliable, the Authors cannot and do not guarantee the accuracy, validity, timeliness, or completeness of any information or data made available to you for any particular purpose. Neither the Authors, nor the Publisher, will be liable or have any responsibility of any kind for any loss or damage that you incur in the event of errors, inaccuracies, or omissions.

Risk   Investing involves risk including possible loss of principal. An investor should consider his or her own investment objectives and risks carefully before investing. There is no guarantee that investments will result in profits or that they will not result in losses. All investors need to fully understand the risks associated with any kind of investing he or she chooses to do. Economic factors, market conditions, and investment strategies will affect the performance of any portfolio and there are no assurances that it will match or outperform any particular benchmark.

No Reliance   The Authors will not be liable, whether in contract, tort (including, but not limited to, negligence) or otherwise, in respect to any damage, expense or other loss you may suffer arising out of or in connection with any information or content provided herein or any reliance you may place upon such information, content, or views. Any investments you make are at your sole discretion and risk.

Disclaimer of Warranty and Limitation of Liability   In no event will the Authors, the Publisher, their affiliates, or any such parties be liable to you for any direct, indirect, special, consequential, incidental, or any other damages of any kind.

Introduction

Why is this book different from all other investing books?

As you have probably noticed, there are quite a few investing books out there. Many of them were written by some of the world's greatest investors. So, why should *you* read *our* book?

Stock investing is more prevalent than ever, whether directly or indirectly through brokerage accounts, exchange-traded funds (ETFs), mutual funds, or retirement plans. Despite this, the vast majority of individual investors have no training on how to pick stocks, let alone basic financial literacy. And, until now, there hasn't been a truly accessible, easy-to-understand resource available to help them. ***The Little Book of Investing Like the Pros***: ***5 Steps for Picking Stocks*** was written to fill this void.

We believe the simplicity and accessibility of our stock picking framework is truly unique. Using real-world examples and actual Wall Street models used by the pros, we teach you how to pick stocks in a highly logical, step-by-step manner. Our goal is straightforward—to impart the skills necessary for finding high-quality stocks while protecting your portfolio with risk management best practices.

Our practical approach is designed to help demystify the investing process, which can be intimidating. This training will help set you apart from others who are largely flying blind.

Pilots require extensive training before receiving a license. Doctors must graduate medical school, followed by a multi-year residency. Even those providing professional investment advice require certification. But, anyone can buy a stock without any training whatsoever. While buying stocks on a hunch and a prayer may not endanger your life, it can certainly put your finances at risk.

In our original best-selling book, ***Investment Banking: Valuation, Leveraged Buyouts, and Mergers & Acquisitions***, we developed a highly practical guide on valuation and corporate finance. Our step-by-step, how-to approach resonated with a broad audience, selling over 200,000 copies and still going strong. While our first book was designed largely for investment bankers, it attracted attention from professional investors.

We also received positive feedback from beginner investors seeking to understand Wall Street valuation techniques. Hardly a day passed without family and friends asking us about popular stocks—e.g., Facebook (FB), Amazon (AMZN), Apple (AAPL), Netflix (NFLX), and Google/Alphabet (GOOG), collectively known as FAANG. A popular line of questioning centered on a stock such as AMZN trading at $1,848 per share vs. FB at $205, with the read-through that FB was a bargain given the lower share price.

Though just one example, the prevalence of this type of thinking was yet another inspiration to write this book. Note: if it's not clear why comparing AMZN and FB on the basis of stock price as opposed to earnings, business model, performance trends, and other key metrics is fundamentally misguided, then this book is definitely for you. And even if you're square on that (and then some), we have a framework to help take you to the next level!

With the help of dozens of seasoned investors, we developed a concise 5-step framework for picking stocks in *The Little Book of Investing Like the Pros*: sourcing investment ideas, identifying the best opportunities, performing due diligence, determining valuation, and making the ultimate go/no-go decision. We also weave in key portfolio construction and risk management techniques. To assist your development, we provide real-world valuation, financial modeling, and portfolio management templates on our website: **www.investinglikethepros.com**

Our 5-step framework is designed to be sufficiently repeatable and flexible for various fundamentals-based investment styles. Most notably, these include value investing, growth, growth at a reasonable price (GARP),[1] long-only, long/short, event-driven/special situations, and distressed. These investment strategies all share the common goal of unearthing stocks with meaningful upside potential, many of which are misunderstood, ignored, or underappreciated by the market.

Our approach towards simplifying the investment process is supported by a playing field that is arguably more level today than ever before. Historically, the discrepancy in access to information between institutional and individual investors provided a tremendous barrier. Individual investors generally didn't know how or where to access relevant data.

Today, all investors have unprecedented access to information and resources thanks to more stringent disclosure requirements and technological developments. There are powerful tools in the public realm to identify, investigate, and execute informed investment decisions. However, proper training on how to use them is critical. That's where our book comes in—namely, a framework for identifying opportunities among the thousands of publicly-traded companies in the market.

---

[1] Companies exhibiting consistent above-market growth coupled with attractive valuation levels.

Successful application of our techniques requires fine-tuning as you gain experience with real-world investment decisions. Over time, you will develop your own distinct style and approach, inevitably borrowing from your professional and personal life. Great stock ideas are often inspired by everyday observations and passions. Your eventual portfolio will likely reflect your educational training, sector expertise, outside interests, and hobbies. Do you have experience in a particular industry? Is there a topic, sector, or trend that fascinates you?

Of course, this is just the beginning of a continuous process. The journey towards becoming a successful investor is by no means easy. Taking the next step will rely upon your own hard work, diligence, judgment, and analytical abilities. You also need to be comfortable with making mistakes early on. Focus on improving your process vs. the outcome. Even pros learn invaluable lessons from their *losers*, often more so than from their *winners*.

In a world where passive investing has proliferated, it merits revisiting the virtues of active investing. Passive investing is exactly as it sounds—you will perform in line with the market/sector, for better or worse. These investment goals work for many. Hence, the arrival of passive investing as a permanent fixture. But, a large portion of investors seek superior returns, which requires an active approach.

The passive approach treats good and bad stocks equally when allocating capital to an index fund or sector ETF. Common sense dictates that a superior approach would target winners and seek to avoid losers to drive above-market returns. For example, as brick-and-mortar retail began to disappear in the face of e-commerce, an ETF tied to the S&P 500 would have kept you invested in an underperforming sector. So, why not use your natural curiosity, smarts, and the tools in our book to aspire to do better?

A quick disclaimer before we get started. While we have sought to distill the highly complex world of investing, we can only simplify so much. Along the way, you will need to research and brush up on some basic terms and concepts. This extends to rudimentary accounting and financial calculations. Proper investing is a serious endeavor and requires real commitment. We believe, however, that the potential rewards are worth the effort.

Structure of the Book

Our book is structured as five chapters that correspond to the five steps in our framework. We use real-world examples throughout to bring these concepts to life.

5-Step Framework

I. Idea Generation

II. Identifying the Best Ideas

III. Business & Financial Due Diligence

IV. Valuation & Catalysts

V. Investment Decision & Portfolio Management

Our flagship case study centers on Delphi Automotive, a global automotive supplier that was the predecessor company to what are now two distinct entities following a tax-free spin in December 2017.[2] Today, these entities trade independently as Aptiv (APTV) and Delphi Technologies (DLPH).

Throughout the book, we focus on the opportunity that investors faced upon Delphi Automotive's initial public offering (IPO) in November 2011. By the time of the company's split in 2017, those who invested from the beginning made nearly five times their money. Using our framework, we take you back in time to illustratively guide you through the process that helped discover, analyze, value, and bless this stock.

Delphi was a textbook restructuring and turnaround opportunity. Before filing for bankruptcy in 2005, it had a fragmented business model with an uncompetitive cost structure and burdensome liabilities. Delphi used the bankruptcy process to rationalize its product lines, sell uncompetitive businesses, and migrate manufacturing to best-cost countries (BCCs). Delphi's lead shareholders,

---

[2] Effective December 2017, Delphi Automotive split into two separate enterprises via a tax-free spin of its Powertrain Segment. This segment was renamed Delphi Technologies. The Electrical/Electronic Architecture and Electronics & Safety segments were rebranded as Aptiv. More on that later ...

Silver Point Capital and Elliott Management, played a key role in the turnaround, working with CEO Rod O'Neal and the management team to transform the company. The reconfigured strategy for the "New Delphi" centered on technology and the three core themes of "Safe, Green and Connected."

Upon emergence, Delphi featured a focused product portfolio, globally cost-competitive structure, and revamped balance sheet. The company also had a concentrated shareholder base that was very active in pursuing value creation. Over time, these core shareholders would be natural sellers as Delphi's stock performed.

As part of their value creation plan, the lead shareholders assembled a world-class Board of Directors, comprised of public company CEOs, auto industry veterans, and highly experienced domain experts (e.g., technology, human resources, capital markets, and M&A). Former DuPont Chairman and CEO Jack Krol was appointed Chairman of the Board and played a critical role. His background as lead director of Tyco International, where he oversaw their successful corporate overhaul, was a key factor in the lead shareholders' decision to bring him on board. He and his fellow directors were instrumental in working with management to develop the strategy around capital allocation, IPO preparation, and messaging to investors.

Delphi also emerged with a more competitive tax regime at the time due to its status as a U.K. tax payer. Add in secular and cyclical tailwinds, a fortified moat, improved financials, and a compelling valuation—in sum, there were multiple ways for an investor to win. There were also many risks to consider. You just had to know what to look for ... and how to do the work.

In late 2011, Delphi went public at a $22 share price. The new strategy would prove enduring over the next several years, persisting long after O'Neal passed the reins to CFO Kevin Clark in 2015. Along the way, there were numerous strategic initiatives that created significant value for shareholders, culminating with the tax-free spin of Delphi's Powertrain Systems segment in 2017.

By the end of 2017, just prior to Delphi's separation into two entities, the stock was trading above $100 per share. Investors who seized upon the opportunity at Delphi's IPO were rewarded with a 375% return. This represented a 30% annualized return vs. the S&P 500 at 13%.

Our 5-step approach to stock picking is designed to help you uncover the next Delphi Automotive. It is also designed to help you manage your stock positions along the way. For example, in 2018, the automotive market began to show signs of a cyclical slowdown. As discussed in the Post-Mortem, the newly spun powertrain business, Delphi

Technologies, also experienced some self-inflicted wounds and headwinds related to its geographic footprint. Our system of early warning signals and active monitoring is crafted to help you avoid these pitfalls. Knowing when to exit or downsize a position is no less important than determining when to enter or upsize.

Step I: Idea Generation

Step I focuses on how professional investors source investment ideas. This process requires a great deal of patience and discipline. It is not uncommon to review dozens, or even hundreds, of companies before a high-quality opportunity is discovered.

Our book focuses on *bottom-up* investing, which is a company-first approach to identifying attractive stocks. You start with the individual company and perform in-depth analysis on its business drivers, financial performance, valuation, and future prospects. We also discuss the *top-down* approach, where you search for opportunities based on macroeconomic ("macro") or secular themes. Key *top-down* strategies center on identifying global or domestic market and business trends/cycles, and buying the beneficiaries. The flip side is to avoid or even short the victims.

Experienced investors tend to incorporate elements of both bottom-up and top-down in their approach. For the bottom-up investor, paying insufficient attention to important macro and other big-picture trends is dangerous. Similarly, the successful top-down investor can't ignore fundamental analysis for individual companies.

In Step I, we discuss the primary buckets from which professional investors source their ideas. We start with undervalued companies for whom there is a path to improved financial performance or a higher valuation. We then focus on companies undertaking value-enhancing corporate actions, such as mergers & acquisitions (M&A), spin-offs & divestitures, restructurings & turnarounds, stock buybacks & dividends, IPOs, and insider buying. Lastly, we explain how to track proven investors to help source new ideas.

Step II: Identifying the Best Ideas

The initial idea search often yields dozens of potential investment opportunities. Step II explains how to parse through a broad list to identify the best ones. This involves a deeper examination of each stock in order to focus your attention on ideas that can become "core" positions. All you need are a few high-quality stocks to kick-start a strong portfolio.

This thinning of the herd relies upon performing high level research on each potential idea in a quick and systematic manner. Towards that end, we provide you with a framework that helps you do just that. It centers on *investment thesis, business model, management team, risks & considerations,* and *financials & valuation.* This preliminary analysis is necessary to separate fool's gold from the "real McCoy."

We also provide a corresponding *investment write-up template* to help you track and organize your research on each stock idea. This template maps to our Step II framework and allows for easy comparison across multiple companies.

The longer the list of potential ideas generated from Step I, the more difficult the task of refining. Sometimes, an idea may jump off the page as a game-changer for your portfolio. In most cases, however, the ideas with the highest upside opportunity are not so black and white. Once the obvious outliers are eliminated, in-depth analysis on the remaining stocks can begin.

Step III: Business & Financial Due Diligence

In Step III, it's time to perform a much deeper dive on those opportunities that survived the culling process. More thorough business and financial research is needed following the early stage vetting. In other words, *this is the key due diligence phase.*

On the business front, we demonstrate how to judge whether a company is high quality, or can become high quality. This involves examining its core strengths as well as the risks that could potentially derail your investment thesis. Much of this work is qualitative, requiring sound judgment and insight. Experience and familiarity with specific business models and sectors is particularly helpful here. Your personal interests and perspectives may also come in handy.

On the financial front, the company's core financial statements need to be thoroughly scrubbed to determine its track record, health, and prospects. A large portion of this analysis is simply making observations about key financial items and seeking defensible answers. You must be acutely aware of any key weaknesses related to growth, margins, FCF, or balance sheet. We also show you how to develop a financial projection model, which serves as the basis for your valuation work in Step IV.

If you can't gain comfort with the business and financial case, then the investment is probably not going to work for you. And that's okay. You don't want to invest in a business you don't understand or believe in. And, you don't want to invest in a company with a weak financial profile that is unlikely to dramatically improve.

Step IV: Valuation & Catalysts

In Step IV, we turn our attention to valuation, arguably the core component of the investment process. Here you need to determine what the company is worth, whether it is cheap or expensive, and whether there are any "catalysts" for revaluation. Even a stock that passes the business and financial test with flying colors may fail the valuation test. In other words, it may be too expensive at current levels to produce an attractive return. This is the trap of "*good company, bad stock*."

In this chapter, we teach you how to perform the key valuation methodologies at the core of any stock analysis. These include market and intrinsic valuation techniques, such as *comparable companies* and *discounted cash flow analysis*. We also discuss M&A valuation approaches, including *precedent transactions, leveraged buyout analysis*, and *accretion/(dilution)*. More nuanced techniques, such as *sum-of-the-parts* and *net asset value*, are then introduced to round out your skill set.

Some combination of these tools is used to determine your *price target* (PT) for a given stock, which is critical for making your ultimate investment decision. Further, we review common catalysts that can unlock the hidden value in a stock and trigger a revaluation. Catalysts may be internally-driven, as part of an evolving management strategy, or external, triggered by shareholder activism or regulatory changes. Key catalysts include earnings beats, M&A, capital return, refinancings, CEO changes, and new product launches.

Step V: Investment Decision & Portfolio Management

You have identified a compelling idea, performed due diligence, and have a view on what the company is worth. All of this informed your all-important price target. It is now time to make the ultimate investment decision. Is the stock a *buy, short, track,* or *pass*?

In the event a buy or short decision is made, the work doesn't stop there. Going forward, the position must be constantly monitored. New developments may materially change the initial investment thesis for better or worse. Effective monitoring involves constant reflection, analysis, and synthesis of events that may impact the underlying business.

Building a sound portfolio requires additional skills beyond just stock picking. Successful portfolio construction involves selecting a collection of stocks tailored to your specific investment goals, strategy, and risk tolerance. This means proper sizing and prioritization of your positions. A large position should reflect its ranking relative to other stocks in the portfolio in terms of overall quality, upside potential (including possible catalysts), and conviction level.

Disciplined investors employ risk management techniques to optimize their portfolios and protect their downside. Key tools include capping exposure levels, as well as setting guidelines for limiting losses and taking profit. Exposure levels refer to individual position sizing, sector concentration, and geographic focus, among others. We also teach you basic techniques for hedging and portfolio stress testing.

Chapter One

Step I:
Idea Generation

~

How do you find investment ideas?

There are tens of thousands of publicly-traded companies on various stock exchanges around the world. So, where do you begin? The search for investment ideas takes many forms. At a basic level, it starts with reading ... a lot. Stay on top of industry standards, such as *Barron's, Bloomberg, Grant's, The Financial Times,* and *The Wall Street Journal,* and broaden from there. Successful investors pay attention to what is going on in the world.

Your search also extends to everyday life and the products and services around you. There are countless stories of people who found great stock ideas inspired by observations from their daily lives. What are people buying? Where are they shopping? What are they talking about? What websites are they visiting?

Many investors take a *bottom-up* approach, which focuses on the fundamentals of individual companies. Within bottom-up, several common sources of investment ideas are prevalent. These include undervalued companies, "earnings compounders," operational improvement and turnaround stories, M&A, spin-offs, restructurings, and capital return. Evaluating these opportunities requires a basic understanding of business drivers, financial analysis, and valuation. You didn't go to business school? Don't worry—bottom-up investing is the primary focus of our book and we've got you covered in the chapters ahead.

Others employ a *top-down* approach, whereby they search for opportunities based on macro or secular themes. These themes are expected to drive accelerated earnings growth and ideally the revaluation of a particular sector. Key macro top-down strategies center on global market trends and business cycles, as well as movements in interest rates, currencies, and commodities. Secular themes include changing consumption patterns, product penetration rates, and demographics, as well as emerging technologies, structural competitive shifts, and regulatory developments.

Experienced investors tend to incorporate elements of both bottom-up and top-down in their approach. Even the most ardent fundamentals-based investors are highly attuned to the macro environment. It is imperative to understand the impact that certain scenarios can have on individual stocks. As the saying goes: "If you don't do macro, macro will do you."

The process of generating ideas requires great patience and discipline. You may need to review hundreds of companies before a high-quality opportunity stands out. Therefore, it is critical to know where to look and what to look for.

While certain techniques are prevalent, each investor develops a distinct style with its own nuances and variations. The experience-based nature of investing means that professional investors tend to fine-tune their idea generation techniques over time. Even the most seasoned pros must evolve and adapt to dynamic market conditions, adding various bells and whistles along the way.

Screens

Screening tools are helpful for efficiently sourcing investment ideas. *Screens* allow you to use customized criteria to sift through large databases of companies to identify stock opportunities. Pros run screens on a regular basis in their continuous search for ideas.

A bottom-up screen might target stocks trading below a specified valuation level or growing above a certain rate. Another might focus on recent M&A transactions, upcoming IPOs, or companies with new share repurchase authorizations (see Exhibit 1.1).

A top-down investor with a thesis on increasing oil prices would screen for energy sector opportunities in combination with financial criteria. Alternatively, a thesis might center on the secular trends of increasing broadband usage or mobile device proliferation. Here, the screen would focus on sub-sectors within Tech, Media & Telecom (TMT) with additional filters for selected financial metrics.

A multitude of stock screening tools are widely available online for free or at relatively low cost (e.g., Yahoo! Finance). At a minimum, you should set up alerts from financial news sources (e.g., Google Alerts, WSJ) that automatically pick up newly announced corporate events. More advanced tools that are highly customizable can be accessed from subscription services, such as Bloomberg.

EXHIBIT 1.1 Screening Output—Buyback Authorizations >5% of Market Cap & Market Cap >$1 billion

($ in millions, except per share data)

New Buyback Authorizations								as of 12/31/2012		
Date Announced	Company	Ticker	Sector	New Buyback Announced	% of Market Cap	Current Share Price	Market Cap	Enterprise Value	Fwd. EV / EBITDA	Fwd. P / E
12/19/12	General Motors	GM	Automotive	$5,500	11%	$28.83	$47,944	$57,252	3.7x	8.2x
12/14/12	MSCI	MSCI	Business Services	$300	8%	$30.99	$3,826	$4,257	10.2x	18.2x
12/13/12	CoreLogic	CLGX	Technology	$250	9%	$26.92	$2,776	$3,396	7.3x	16.0x
12/10/12	Graphic Packaging	GPK	Packaging	$300	12%	$6.46	$2,572	$4,511	7.1x	14.4x
12/7/12	Lennox International	LII	Industrials	$300	11%	$52.52	$2,705	$3,137	9.1x	14.7x
12/6/12	Sirius XM	SIRI	Satellite Radio	$2,000	11%	$2.89	$19,009	$20,888	16.1x	19.9x
11/9/12	Skyworks Solutions	SWKS	Semiconductors	$200	5%	$20.30	$3,907	$3,579	7.0x	9.5x
11/7/12	Babcock & Wilcox	BWC	Electrical Equipment	$250	8%	$26.20	$3,107	$2,772	6.1x	11.4x
11/5/12	Dover Corporation	DOV	Machinery	$1,000	8%	$65.71	$12,086	$13,487	7.8x	12.6x
10/23/12	Airgas	ARG	Chemicals	$600	8%	$91.29	$7,202	$9,245	10.0x	19.8x
9/26/12	Alaska Air	ALK	Airlines	$250	8%	$43.09	$3,097	$2,978	3.4x	8.5x
8/13/12	Xilinx	XLNX	Semiconductors	$750	8%	$35.86	$9,692	$8,901	11.3x	16.9x

Bottom-Up Approach

Bottom-up investing is a company-first approach to identifying attractive stocks. You start with the individual company and perform in-depth analysis on its business drivers, financial performance, valuation, and future prospects. This type of work forms the basis of traditional stock picking.

Common bottom-up investment strategies include long-only, long/short, and event-driven/special situations. Others focus on specific sectors or geographies. The long-only strategy is centered on buying and holding a portfolio of quality stocks, often with a long-term perspective. Long/short layers in a shorting strategy to protect against specific stock or sector risks, overall market risk, or to produce returns in its own right (see Chapter 5). An event-driven/special situations strategy focuses on corporate actions such as M&A, spin-offs, and buybacks.

As shown in Exhibit 1.2, certain areas have proven to be fruitful for sourcing quality investment ideas. For example, "value investors" tend to focus on undervalued stocks that are misunderstood by the market. Stock pickers also look for companies undertaking shareholder-friendly activities, such as buybacks, M&A, and management upgrades.

EXHIBIT 1.2 Bottom-Up Approach

Bottom-Up Approach

- Valuation

- Financial Performance

- Mergers & Acquisitions

- Spin-offs & Divestitures

- Restructurings & Turnarounds

- Buybacks & Dividends

- Initial Public Offerings

- Insider Buying & Ownership

- Tracking Successful Investors & Activists

- **Valuation** – traditional valuation screens seek to identify stocks that are "cheap," usually on the basis of a valuation multiple. It is, however, important to distinguish between companies that are cheap because they are misunderstood vs. those that deserve to be.

- **Financial Performance** – financial metrics and trends are critical for identifying potential winners and losers. Improving fundamentals may signal a compelling investment opportunity, e.g., accelerating growth rates, expanding profit margins, deleveraging, and improving returns. Companies with inferior margins vs. peers merit analysis on whether they can close the gap.

- **Mergers & Acquisitions** – M&A can create substantial long-term value for shareholders. This is especially true when acquirers undertake transformational acquisitions or "bolt-ons" that are *accretive* and portfolio enhancing. Identifying sectors "in play" can lead to opportunities among both acquirers and targets.

- **Spin-offs & Divestitures** – transactions where a company "spins" (distributes to existing shareholders), IPOs, or sells one or more of its businesses/divisions. Spin-offs and divestitures aim to unlock or highlight the full value of distinct businesses currently under one corporate umbrella.

- **Restructurings & Turnarounds** – restructurings are situations where a company emerges from bankruptcy/reorganization with a public equity listing, typically accompanied by a stronger balance sheet. Turnaround situations exist outside of formal bankruptcies and restructurings. Any troubled company represents an opportunity to explore the potential for dramatic improvement.

- **Buybacks & Dividends** – two main methods for returning cash to shareholders. For buybacks, companies engaging in first-time, systematic, or substantial share repurchases (e.g., >5% of the public float annually) are particularly interesting. For dividends, new initiations, sizable yields, or increasing payout ratios[1] merit exploration.

- **Initial Public Offerings** – first-time public offerings by companies, including those owned by private equity (PE)[2] and venture capital (VC) firms. Often, these companies are offered at a discount to peers and may not be well-understood by the market due to lack of a public track record or comps.

---

[1] Refers to the percentage of net income paid out as a dividend.
[2] Alternative asset managers that traditionally acquire companies through leveraged buyouts (LBOs).

- **Insider Buying & Ownership** – senior executive(s) purchasing substantial stock in their company may signal that the shares are undervalued or there is significant value creation ahead. Correspondingly, proven CEOs that have large financial incentives to improve performance deserve attention.

- **Tracking Successful Investors & Activists** – reviewing public filings for a select group of investors with strong track records can uncover buying opportunities. The SEC[3] requires investment funds with $100 million or greater in assets under management (AUM) to disclose their equity holdings on a quarterly basis in a Schedule 13-F filing.[4]

---

[3] U.S. Securities and Exchange Commission.

[4] The 13-F lists a fund's holdings, including the amount of shares held. It must be filed within 45 days after quarter end.

Valuation

When performing valuation screens, you need to go beyond just finding "cheap" stocks. A simple screen for companies trading at under 15x price-to-earnings (P/E) will invariably produce a large output. And you likely won't be much closer to finding an undervalued stock. Most of these companies are cheap for good reason.

The key is to find stocks that are cheap because they are misunderstood and you believe their earnings will accelerate and/or the market will "re-rate" them higher—that is, afford them a higher multiple. You must do this while avoiding so-called "value traps," i.e., stocks that appear cheap but are discounted for a reason. They may even be overpriced due to fundamental or structural challenges that threaten future earnings.

Alternatively, you may find stocks that do not appear cheap on a multiples basis or vs. peers, but have a clear path to outperformance. For example, a high-growth company trading at 20x P/E may prove more interesting than a slower-growth peer trading at 17.5x. Assuming the 20x company is growing earnings at 25% per year, its implied P/E off Year 3 earnings is only 10x. Meanwhile, assuming the 17.5x peer is growing earnings at 10% per year, its Year 3 P/E is 13x and therefore more expensive.

Often, the bottom-up approach is combined with top-down to design an effective valuation screen. For example, you may look for cheap stocks in a sector undergoing a major secular shift or cyclical rebound.

Common valuation screens include:

- **Trading at a low absolute or relative value** – a company whose valuation looks compelling given the business fundamentals and outlook. This may be on a relative basis vs. peers or its own historical levels (e.g., a significant discount to its 52-week or all-time high). Valuation is typically measured and compared on the basis of trading multiples. Key multiples include any combination of P/E, price-to-free cash flow (P/FCF),[5] price-to-book (P/B), and enterprise value-to-EBITDA[6] (EV/EBITDA), among others.

---

[5] The inverse of P/FCF, known as FCF yield (FCF/S-to-share price), is often used by investors.

[6] EBITDA (<u>e</u>arnings <u>b</u>efore <u>i</u>nterest, <u>t</u>axes, <u>d</u>epreciation, and <u>a</u>mortization) is a widely-used proxy for operating cash flow as it reflects a company's total cash operating costs for producing its products and services.

- **Compelling valuation relative to growth** – the P/E-to-growth ratio (PEG) is key here. Defined as P/E ratio divided by earnings growth rate, it is designed to measure a stock's value proposition relative to its growth prospects. A lower PEG ratio may indicate that a stock is undervalued. As discussed above, a stock with a 20x P/E ratio and 25% earnings per share (EPS) growth (PEG of 0.8x) should be more compelling than one at 17.5x and 10% growth (PEG of 1.75x).

- **High returns with low valuation** – return on capital metrics, most notably return on invested capital (ROIC),[7] are a key indicator of quality. The ideal opportunity combines high and improving returns with a low current valuation. High returns can be put to work by investing in growth projects and/or returning capital to shareholders.

---

[7] Often defined as tax-effected EBIT (earnings before interest and taxes) or EBIAT (earnings before interest after taxes) *divided* by net PP&E (property, plant and equipment) *plus* working capital. Tax-effected EBIT and EBIAT may also be referred to as NOPAT (net operating profit after taxes).

Financial Performance

A company's financial performance should be reflected in its share price, for better or worse. Accelerating top and bottom-line growth rates should be rewarded with strong share price performance. The opposite should hold true for decelerating trends.

The same rules apply to other key financial metrics, such as profit margins, FCF generation, and return on capital. Sometimes, however, the market fails to adequately recognize improving financial performance. Similarly, underperformance on a relative basis—e.g., lower margins or returns vs. peers—should be explored as a potential turnaround opportunity.

Capital structure typically goes hand in hand with financial performance. Here, you want to focus on the amount and cost of a company's debt, when the debt comes due, and the ability to service interest payments. As with operating performance, strengthening credit statistics can help drive the stock price.

The above-mentioned metrics need to be viewed on both an absolute and relative basis vs. peers. Screening services provide countless variations for identifying financial performance trends.

Common financial performance screens include:

- **Growth** – arguably the most important driver of valuation. Consistent growth in sales and earnings is a classic indicator of quality. These so-called earnings compounders that deliver year-in and year-out are the traditional stock picker's bread and butter, and tend to receive a premium valuation. While all growth is celebrated, organic is preferred over M&A-driven.

- **Margins** – expanding or declining profit margins are telltale signs of company performance. Margin expansion tends to indicate pricing power, cost control, and power over suppliers. Margin erosion can be a warning sign of key business challenges. Investors focus on gross profit, EBITDA, operating profit (EBIT),[8] and net income margins.

- **FCF Generation** – professional investors focus on a company's ability to generate cash, which can be used to fund organic growth projects, M&A, capital return to shareholders, or repay debt. Companies that convert a meaningful percentage of net income into FCF are held in high regard. Key metrics include FCF conversion (FCF-to-net income or EBITDA) and FCF margin (FCF-to-sales).

---

[8] EBIT is often the same as *operating profit* or *income from operations* on a company's reported income statement. It is similar to EBITDA, but nets out depreciation & amortization (D&A) expenses, and therefore may better reflect capital intensity.

- **Return Metrics** – measure a company's ability to provide earnings (or returns) to capital providers. These ratios employ a metric of profitability (e.g., EBIAT, NOPAT, or net income) in the numerator and capital (e.g., invested capital, total assets, or shareholders' equity) in the denominator. Return metrics measure how efficiently management deploys capital. Ideally, companies should have an ROIC that exceeds its *cost of capital* (see Chapter 4), which indicates an ability to deliver excess returns to shareholders.

- **Capital Structure** – helps drive stock price performance in many ways. Balance sheet capacity can be tapped to fund growth projects, M&A, or return capital. It also provides support and liquidity during difficult times as equity investors learned during the 2008/09 financial crisis (a.k.a., the "Great Recession"). Key metrics include debt-to-EBITDA ("leverage") and EBITDA-to-interest expense ("coverage"). Improving credit metrics may be due to strengthening financial performance and/or debt repayment.

Mergers & Acquisitions

M&A refers broadly to the purchase and sale of businesses. The decision to buy all or part of another company is driven by numerous factors. Paramount among these is the desire to grow or improve an existing platform through new products, customers, end markets, or geographies. M&A may also take the form of expansion into entirely new business lines. Growth through M&A often represents a cheaper, faster, and safer option than building a business from scratch.

An M&A-centric approach to identifying investment opportunities can be compelling. Screening for sizable new deals is a good place to start. This often leads you to identify sectors "in play," where both potential targets and acquirers may be interesting opportunities. For potential targets, investors focus on natural take-out candidates, especially those trading at 52-week lows or cheap multiples vs. peers. For acquirers, proven management teams with strong M&A track records stand out, especially those with an abundance of cash or low leverage.

Before we dive deeper, a quick disclaimer: M&A has a decidedly mixed track record over the years. Typical traps include over-paying, misguided strategic bets, incompatible cultures, over-leveraging the balance sheet, and poor integration. Each of these individually can be value-destroying, and together they are devastating. So, proceed with caution.

Specific strategies centered on M&A activity include:

- **Transformational Deals** – acquirers undertaking transactions that are sizable, strategic, and synergistic. *Typical Screens*: recently announced or closed deals representing at least 10% of the acquirer's pre-deal value

- **Sector Consolidation** – sectors in play where both potential target and acquirer share prices can benefit. *Typical Screens*: sector deal volumes, both number and size of deals

- **Natural Targets** – companies with logical strategic or PE buyers. *Typical Screens*: pure plays in combination with low valuation multiples or trading near a 52-week low

- **Proven Acquirers** – management teams with successful track records of consummating accretive transactions. *Typical Screens*: active acquirers in terms of volume and dollar amount of deals, often in combination with key balance sheet metrics such as large cash balances or low leverage

Transformational Deals

Transformational deals may be defined by size or strategy, often both. These deals materially move the needle for the acquirer in terms of sales and earnings, as well as strategic direction. They also tend to be highly synergistic due to cost savings and growth opportunities. In some cases, they may result in a valuation re-rating where the acquirer is rewarded with a higher multiple.

You should screen for newly announced or closed deals above a certain threshold. Then review each acquirer's press release and investor presentation. These resources typically provide a deal description, synergy amounts, earnings accretion (or assumptions to perform the calculation), and strategic benefits of the transaction.

Regardless of the level of disclosure, you ultimately must make your own assumptions and judgments on the deal's financial and strategic merits. These will be reflected in your earnings accretion / (dilution) model that analyzes the quantitative effects of the transaction (see Chapter 4). Investors applaud deals that are materially accretive to EPS or FCF/S, ideally by 10% or more on a *pro forma* (PF) basis.

In August 2016, ski resorts operator Vail Resorts (MTN) purchased competitor Whistler Blackcomb (WB CN) for $1.2 billion (13x EV/EBITDA, or 9x on a synergies-adjusted basis). This was a sizable transaction against MTN's then

$5.8 billion enterprise value. Reflective of synergies, the deal was comfortably accretive to EPS.

Whistler was considered one of the most iconic resorts in North America and had a long history of healthy financial performance. The deal expanded Vail's already strong network of mountains into the Canadian market, which buffered some of the seasonality of the overall business given Whistler operates year-round.

A combination of immediate revenue and cost synergies, increasing adoption of season passes, and sharing of best practices was applauded by the market. MTN increased 8% upon deal announcement. Two years later, Vail shareholders had doubled their money. Clearly, this transformational deal delivered transformational returns.

Sector Consolidation

A sector in the midst of consolidation provides fertile ground for M&A-themed ideas. Share prices for both potential targets and acquirers may creep up in anticipation of value-enhancing transactions. This creates a potential win/win situation. Ideally, you want to start investing during the early stages of the consolidation phase to maximize returns.

We recommend screening for newly announced or closed deals and then sorting them by sector. A sector with heavy activity would suggest a *bona fide* consolidation play. The next level of analysis is to find those sector players most likely to transact. This requires a deep understanding of natural targets and acquirers.

A typical narrative might involve a proven acquirer with a stated M&A agenda and a large cash balance. It may also have just lost out on buying someone else and is keen to find a new target. You can then perform high level analysis on fit and synergies with a variety of potential targets.

Clear targets would have an attractive valuation and strategic fit for potential suitors. Social and governance issues are also important. Does the target company have an activist shareholder? Is its Board and management team likely to support a sale of the company?

The global brewing sector presents an interesting case study. In the early 2000s, the industry was highly fragmented with the top five players holding 25% market share. A decade later, after over a dozen sizable deals, their combined market share was well over 50%. Along the way, shareholders for both targets and acquirers made outsized returns. Notable deals included InBev's $61 billion acquisition of Anheuser-Busch in 2008 and SABMiller's acquisition of Foster's for $12 billion in 2011. These two global brewing giants then combined in 2016 to form a $200 billion market cap company.

Natural Targets

A classic M&A investment strategy centers on finding natural takeover candidates. Companies with large competitors looking to expand are at the top of the list. Ditto for companies with unique assets or technologies that would provide a clean plug-and-play for an industry peer.

A clear target might be a small pure play with a modest multiple or trading near a 52-week low. A CEO near retirement with a generous exit package would lend further credibility.[9] Or, perhaps the company is cheap enough or generates enough FCF to attract interest from a PE firm.

It takes two to tango, however. So, you also need to understand the potential buyers. Are the logical buyers in acquisition mode? Are their balance sheets strong enough for sizable M&A? Is a PE buyer likely to be interested?

While backing proven acquirers can be an effective strategy, the target is typically the safer bet upfront. Historically, the takeover premium for public companies has averaged 30% to 40%. In some cases, including bidding wars or hostile takeovers, the premium is much higher. Correctly picking a takeover candidate can provide an outsized return in a short period of time.

---

[9] The age and financial package for senior executives is disclosed in the company's annual proxy statement filed with the SEC.

Former investment bankers have a key advantage in this regard as they understand M&A mechanics, dynamics, and motivations.

In March 2016, Valspar (VAL) was acquired by Sherwin-Williams (SHW) for $113 per share in an all-cash deal to create the largest global player in paints and coatings. This represented a 41% premium to VAL's share price, and a 28% premium to its all-time high. Including the assumption of debt, the total purchase price was $11.3 billion (15x EV/EBITDA, or 11x on a synergies-adjusted basis).

As the #5 global coatings producer in an industry where scale matters, there were multiple logical acquirers for Valspar. Its brand portfolio, strong Asia-Pacific exposure, and history of innovation and technological expertise further enhanced its attractiveness. In short, the clues were all there for investors looking to back a natural takeover candidate.

For Sherwin-Williams, the deal diversified its customer base and geographic exposure, while adding complementary products and capabilities. From a financial perspective, the transaction was highly synergistic and 20% accretive to EPS. SHW shareholders were handsomely rewarded with a 115% return from announcement date through the end of 2019, more than double that of the S&P 500 over the same period.

Proven Acquirers

Proven acquirers refer to companies with demonstrated track records of consummating accretive, value-enhancing deals. In good times, M&A augments underlying solid performance. In difficult times, M&A helps offset sales and earnings headwinds.

Proven acquirer stocks often trade up when they announce a deal. These companies feature highly competent CEOs and in-house M&A professionals, often former investment bankers. A typical playbook would be to acquire peers with lagging margins that can be improved under new management. Proven acquirers have a time-tested integration playbook that is part of the corporate DNA. This enables them to successfully execute and integrate, delivering additional value above and beyond the purchase price.

Orbia Advance Corporation SAB (ORBIA), formerly Mexichem SAB, a global chemical company based in Mexico City, Mexico began a series of strategic acquisitions in early 2007. As part of its initiative to grow its downstream business and diversify geographically, the company acquired Grupo Amanco, AlphaGary, Wavin, and Dura-Line over the next several years. This M&A-driven strategy proved highly profitable for shareholders. By fall of 2014, Mexichem's share price had increased from approximately P$7 to P$56, an eight-fold return in eight years.

So, what's the catch? Is investing in successful serial acquirers too good to be true? Well, there are several risks. To start, this strategy requires a large pipeline of actionable targets. It is also dependent upon the availability of attractive debt financing markets. Furthermore, reliable analysis of serial acquirers' underlying financial performance may prove challenging given the various moving pieces.

Lastly, a proven acquirer's stock may already be priced for perfection. Investor expectations for continued successful deals may be sky high, setting the stage for disappointment.

Spin-offs & Divestitures

A *spin-off* occurs when a parent company (ParentCo) IPOs or distributes shares of one of its business segments (SpinCo) to existing shareholders. Post-spin, the new SpinCo is independent from ParentCo with its own management team, Board of Directors, and shareholders. Spin-offs are headline news items in the financial press and, hence, easy to screen for.

Spin-offs can be fruitful for stock pickers. After all, the premise for separating the businesses is to unlock shareholder value. The implied values of the individual businesses should be greater than the existing consolidated ParentCo. Otherwise, why go through the expense and hassle of the spin-off? The same holds true for the sale or divestiture of non-core or underperforming businesses.

Post-separation, both ParentCo and SpinCo may present meaningful upside potential and need to be assessed independently. For ParentCo, shedding a non-core, neglected business may re-rate the stock. For SpinCo, which is often a lower-quality or capital-starved business, there is perhaps even greater opportunity. Typically, SpinCo's stock comes under immediate selling pressure as the shareholder base turns over. Larger asset managers tend to shy away from smaller illiquid stocks, so they punt them.

Furthermore, the valuation of the newly independent SpinCo tends to suffer from a general lack of information and interest. Newly public entities often trade at a discount due to being unproven with no independent track record. They also tend to have limited research coverage at the onset, particularly if SpinCo is a small-cap stock. These attributes—unwarranted selling pressure, valuation discount, and information asymmetry—can create a compelling scenario.

For *divestitures*, the opportunity lies with ParentCo. After all, the chief motivation for the sale of a non-core or underperforming business is to unlock value. This is classic "addition by subtraction." Divesting a lesser business should lend to a multiple re-rating through an improved product mix. The allocation of sale proceeds towards higher value initiatives or debt paydown should also be a positive for the share price.

In July 2010, Northrop Grumman (NOC) announced it was exploring the sale or spin of its naval shipbuilding business, now trading as Huntington Ingalls (HII). At the time, the industry backdrop was unfavorable given expectations for defense spending cuts. NOC was also trading at a large discount to peers.

Fortunately, both NOC and HII had strong positions on "mission critical" platforms that were difficult for the government to cut. At spin announcement, NOC's share price was $50. By the end of 2019, it had reached $344. Plus, those NOC shareholders who held onto their HII stock distribution realized over $40 of additional value. This equated to a total implied value of nearly $400 per share, representing a nearly 600% return, or 20%+ on an annualized basis.[10]

Restructurings & Turnarounds

Restructuring situations refer to companies that have emerged from bankruptcy or a similar reorganization event. The owners of these companies are typically former debt and equity holders, as well as new investors from credit and distressed funds. Many of them likely purchased the company's debt during financial distress and gained

---

[10] NOC shareholders received one share of HII stock for every six shares of NOC stock owned.

ownership once that debt was converted to equity. As such, they have a low cost basis and are natural sellers seeking to monetize their holdings via a sale or IPO/relisting.[11]

Upon relisting, these companies tend to be neglected or misunderstood by the market given their former troubles. In this sense, they are like spin-offs except with a checkered past. And, like spin-offs, they are easy to screen for and often present intriguing investment opportunities.

Many of these companies have a solid underlying business. The restructuring event may have been triggered by an imprudent debt load, a one-time shock/event, or mismanagement. The solution to the problem typically depends on the cause. An overly aggressive capital structure can be cured by a cleaned-up balance sheet. An uncompetitive cost structure may be fixed with a comprehensive cost-cutting program. Poor execution can be rectified by new management. A fundamentally flawed business model, however, should be treated with extreme caution.

Turnaround situations also exist outside of formal bankruptcies and restructurings. In a broader sense, any troubled company represents an opportunity to dig in and explore the potential for dramatic improvement. Many

---

[11] A relisting occurs when a formerly public company that went bankrupt or was delisted reemerges on an exchange without a formal IPO.

turnarounds are led by a new CEO or active shareholder. An outsider can often provide fresh perspective and bold leadership to implement change.

Tropicana Entertainment (TPCA), the casino operator, is a prototypical restructuring and turnaround story. Columbia Sussex purchased the company in January 2007 for $2.8 billion, loading it up with debt heading into the Great Recession. Less than a year later, Tropicana was stripped of its license in Atlantic City by NJ state regulators due to proposed major cost-cuts and layoffs that were deemed excessive. By May 2008, Tropicana filed for bankruptcy, forced to fold its bad hand of deteriorating market conditions, high leverage, and operational missteps.

And yet, the iconic Tropicana brand and its casino properties never died. In many ways, this was a classic case of "*good company, bad balance sheet.*" During Chapter 11, the company shed nearly $2.5 billion of debt and successfully renewed its gaming licenses. In March 2010, Tropicana emerged from bankruptcy in a $200 million deal backed by Carl Icahn. By November 2010, Tropicana relisted on the OTC Markets (over-the-counter) at $14 per share.

Over the next several years, Tropicana made major investments in new and existing assets, including renovations and upgrades, hotel room improvements, and additional resort amenities. Tropicana also consummated a major M&A transaction in 2014, buying Lumière in St. Louis, MO for $260 million. By 2018, EBITDA had improved from roughly $45 million upon bankruptcy emergence to nearly $200 million.

The story concluded in April 2018 when Tropicana agreed to sell its real estate assets to Gaming and Leisure Properties (GLPI) and merge its gaming and hotel operations into Eldorado Resorts (ERI) for a total of $1.85 billion. This implied a $73.50 share price, equating to a 425% return since the relisting, or 23% on an annualized basis.

Another notable turnaround story centered on Charter Communications (CHTR). In December 2011, Tom Rutledge was announced as the new CEO, inheriting a recently-bankrupt, capital-starved cable company facing competitive pressures. Rutledge came from industry peer Cablevision (CVC) where he drove sector-leading operating metrics, took FCF from approximately -$375 million to +$685 million, and delivered annualized returns in the high teens. CHTR's share price reacted favorably to the news of his hiring, increasing 5% that day.

Under Rutledge, Charter immediately embarked on a capital investment program to improve its network. The company also simplified its pricing plans and focused on improving customer service. Within a year, CHTR announced a highly accretive bolt-on acquisition, followed by the simultaneous acquisitions of Time Warner Cable and

Bright House Networks roughly two years later. Investors who identified the opportunity in Charter on Day 1 were rewarded with a nearly 675% return, or approximately 30% annualized through 2019.

Like restructurings and bankruptcies, potential turnarounds must be handled with extreme care. The Tropicana and Charter success stories are the exception, not the norm. Many troubled companies never turn around. In fact, their troubles often intensify and result in chronic under-performance and even bankruptcy.

Buybacks & Dividends

Efficient capital allocators tend to outperform peers over time and create catalysts when they announce substantial buyback authorizations or large dividends. Lesser companies might hoard cash or embark on undisciplined M&A in the absence of attractive internal growth projects.

For interesting potential buyback situations, screen for companies that authorize large share repurchase programs (e.g., > 5% of market cap). This may signal that management believes their stock is undervalued. At the very least, it conveys confidence in the company's prospects. Of course, the mere announcement of such a program does not signal an "all clear" to pile in.

You need to review management's buyback track record. Has the company historically repurchased stock at attractive prices? Has it been a meaningful value creation lever? Or, was it simply a mechanism to meet earnings expectations/guidance[12] or offset dilution from employee stock compensation?

First-time buyback announcements require particular scrutiny. Will the company actually follow through on the authorization? Does management believe the stock is undervalued or is it a signal that they are unable to find attractive growth projects? Beware the latter as it may portend slowing earnings or future multiple compression.

Another buyback screen centers on identifying companies with sizable share count reductions over set periods of time (e.g., prior three or five years). Companies with a successful share repurchase track record tend to be rewarded.

Sirius XM (SIRI), the satellite radio company, has created substantial shareholder value over time through systematic buybacks. From 2013 through 2018, SIRI repurchased $10.8 billion of stock, or $1.8 billion per year on average. To put this in perspective, SIRI's market cap was only $15 billion when its buyback program was originally

---

[12] Providing guidance is discretionary on the part of the company; it is not an SEC requirement.

announced in December 2012. This aggressive return of capital helped Sirius XM grow FCF/S at a 20%+ CAGR.[13] Correspondingly, SIRI's share price surpassed $7 by mid-2018 from a starting point of $2.79 in late 2012.

For dividends, common screens center on stocks with yields greater than a target threshold, e.g., 2.5%. *Dividend yield* is defined as a company's annual dividend per share divided by its share price. A company with a $50 stock price and $1.25 in dividends per share has a 2.5% yield. A low dividend yield (e.g., 1% or lower) and no clear path to a substantial increase is not exciting. Consistent and growing dividend stocks, on the other hand, are revered. Companies that have raised dividends for at least 25 consecutive years are known as "dividend aristocrats."

While targeting proven dividend champions is a common strategy, there is opportunity on the other end of the spectrum. Namely, cash rich or underleveraged companies that have refrained from such activity in the past. These companies merit attention upon new dividend initiations or sizable increases in payout ratios. Beware, however, companies whose annual dividend payment consistently exceeds FCF, especially those who fund the gap with incremental debt.

---

[13] Compound annual growth rate = (Ending Value / Beginning Value) ^ (1 / (Ending Year - Beginning Year)) - 1.

Initial Public Offerings

IPOs represent a company's introduction to public equity investors. As such, IPO candidates tend to be relatively unknown in terms of the strength of their business model and financial performance. Furthermore, new IPOs do not receive equity research coverage until after an initial 10-day "quiet period."[14] This information and time gap provides an opportunity for potential investors to find true differentiation.

Moreover, IPOs often price at a significant discount to the company's implied market value vs. peers (typically 15% or more). The discount affords additional cushion for investors to "get the story right."

The information mismatch inherent in IPOs is greatest for candidates without an obvious public comparable. In these cases, a little extra work can pay off as others avoid an unknown entity lacking a clear public valuation marker. Of course, this risk is real as the market has not yet "spoken" on how such companies should be valued.

---

[14] While the SEC mandatory quiet period is 10 days, most banks still adhere to the prior 25-day rule. Issuers with < $1.07 billion in sales, a.k.a., EGCs (emerging growth companies) are exempt. The quiet period does not apply to banks who did not participate in the offering.

Returning to Delphi from the Intro Chapter, the company's November 2011 IPO price of $22 implied a 2013E[15] EV/EBITDA of 3.5x, P/E of 5x, and FCF yield of nearly 15%. This represented a substantial discount to other secular grower auto parts suppliers, who were trading at roughly 6x EV/EBITDA, 11x P/E, and a 7.5% FCF yield, respectively (see Chapter 4, Exhibit 4.3). Rather, the market was pricing Delphi in line with so-called production-linked suppliers, whose fortunes were tied largely to auto unit volumes.

As Delphi performed, the market began to recognize its powerful secular growth dynamics tied to new product adoption, increasing content per vehicle, and accelerating profitability. Accordingly, its bankruptcy stigma began to fade and new investors entered the stock. Prior to the spin transaction in late 2017, Delphi's share price surpassed $100. Its EV/EBITDA, P/E, and FCF yield had improved to approximately 12x, 18x, and 4%, respectively. We give more color on how this transpired in the chapters to follow.

---

[15] E stands for "estimated."

Insider Buying & Ownership

A company's senior management should have better insight into their business and its prospects than anyone else. That is their job, quite literally what they are paid to focus on all day, every day. Therefore, management purchases and sales of company stock may signal possible entry and exit points for investors. As Peter Lynch pointed out: "Insiders might sell their shares for any number of reasons, but they buy them for only one—they think the price will rise."

Changes in ownership by a U.S. public company's officers and directors require the filing of a Form 4 with the SEC. Your stock alerts should inform you when these hit the wire. Sizable purchases and sales also get picked up by major financial news and business publications. Insider purchases are traditionally a bullish signal, while large sales may portend trouble ahead.

J.P. Morgan's (JPM) CEO Jamie Dimon has been particularly adept at buying his company's stock. In January 2009, he purchased 500,000 shares of JPM at an average price of $23, equating to $11.5 million. His purchase in the midst of the global financial crisis was front-page business news, signaling confidence in JPM shares after they fell more than 50% over the prior two years. In the twelve months following Dimon's purchase, the stock increased 90%. Those who were paying attention and followed his lead would have nearly doubled their money in a year.

Likewise, in July 2012, amidst Eurozone sovereign concerns, Dimon again injected personal capital into JPM, buying an additional 500,000 shares at $34 for $17 million. A year later, JPM was up 63%. Then, in February 2016, with the market retreating on China concerns and plunging oil prices, Dimon again stepped in. He bought another 500,000 shares at $53 for $26.5 million, reassuring JPM shareholders and the broader market along the way. Twelve months later, the stock was up 64%. By the end of 2019, JPM's share price was nearly $140. Investing behind Dimon's insider buying would have proven highly profitable.

A related strategy centers on backing companies whose CEOs have significant stock ownership and stand to benefit materially from share price appreciation. This includes CEOs who have options with exercise prices at substantial premiums to the current share price.

The notion that CEO compensation and shareholder rewards should be closely aligned is intuitive. First popularized by economist Michael Jensen in the mid-1970s, a higher percentage of executive compensation in the form of stock has become commonplace. This has replaced the old model where CEOs were positioned to receive a large cash salary and bonus with relatively little "skin in the game."

Tracking Successful Investors & Activists

The 13-Fs for a select group of investors can be insightful for sourcing ideas. Closely-watched portfolios include those of Warren Buffett of Berkshire Hathaway, David Abrams of Abrams Capital, Stan Druckenmiller of Duquesne, Andreas Halvorsen of Viking Global, Seth Klarman of The Baupost Group, Nelson Peltz of Trian Fund Management, and Paul Singer of Elliott Management, to name a few. These investors have outstanding long-term track records and are known for performing deep due diligence on their stock positions.

Keep in mind, however, that 13-Fs are filed with a 45-day lag after quarter end. For some of these holdings, the optimal entry point may have passed by the time of disclosure. Or, the positions may have even turned over by the filing date. Therefore, you may want to focus on recent investments where the share price has not yet appreciated.

When a person or group accumulates an ownership stake of greater than 5% in a company, they are required to file a Schedule 13-D within ten days, or 13-G within 45 days. A 13-D represents an active position whereby the holders plan to engage in strategic discussions with management. A 13-G represents a passive stake. Both filings indicate high conviction in a stock's upside potential.

Activist investors are change agents and target situations accordingly. In some cases, they accelerate transformational events that may have been identified long ago by existing investors. Therefore, these same shareholders typically cheer a credible activist's entrance. Activists also tend to attract new investors, which provides an immediate share price pop. Long-term upside is determined by the activist's success in initiating change as well as the results of the strategic moves themselves.

In April 2013, Microsoft (MSFT) was trading below $30 per share when activist investor ValueAct Capital confirmed it had taken a $2 billion stake. While this represented less than 1% of the shares outstanding, it was clear that ValueAct was intent on driving change. On the day the stake was announced, MSFT rose over 3%, and then climbed to nearly $35 by the end of May.

Prior to ValueAct's entry, Microsoft's share price had been largely stagnant since 1998. Concerns were percolating over CEO Steve Ballmer and the company's strategy, most notably a misguided foray into devices and falling behind Apple and Google in mobile computing. By August 2013, Ballmer announced that he would retire and ValueAct secured a Board seat. This was the beginning of more dramatic changes on the horizon ...

In September 2013, Microsoft authorized a new $40 billion share repurchase program vs. a then $450 billion market cap, and raised its dividend by over 20%. By February 2014, Ballmer was replaced by 20-year Microsoft veteran Satya Nadella. In the coming years, Nadella would impart sizable cultural and strategic changes, including less emphasis on traditional desktop software and more focus on cloud, enterprise, and mobile.

Nadella's strategy reinvigorated Microsoft's financial performance. A combination of strong commercial cloud growth, improved product mix, and transitioning the enterprise business towards a subscription model was applauded by investors. By the time ValueAct exited their position in the first quarter of 2018, MSFT's share price was above $90, or 200% higher.

Of course, tracking other investors requires adhering to the usual cautions. Beware the groupthink that may result in ill-fated "hedge fund hotels." Some investors shy away entirely from following others, seeking to avoid "crowded" trades. For those being followed, their positions may benefit from copycat demand.

Top-Down Approach

The top-down approach to investing targets stocks expected to benefit from macro or secular tailwinds. These trends are meant to drive sustained earnings growth and valuation multiple expansion. Ideally, they also protect the core business against adverse economic conditions and market shocks. Even during stormy times, you want the wind blowing at your back, not in your face.

The power of macro themes is evident every day where statements and actions by central banks move markets. Investors focus particularly on the U.S. Federal Reserve ("Fed"), European Central Bank (ECB), Bank of Japan (BOJ), and People's Bank of China (PBOC). Macro factors underscored the long bull-run following the Great Recession. Low interest rates and easy monetary policy helped drive stocks to record levels.

Secular themes are abundant in an age of fast-moving change. This applies to old-world and new-world sectors alike. A top-down investor might mine the auto sector for ideas related to electrification and autonomy of vehicles. Similarly, 21st century secular themes around e-commerce, the cloud, the sharing economy, and social media have proven highly rewarding.

Much of top-down idea generation stems from old-fashioned research. Read and watch traditional news sources, including financial, economic, and sector-specific media. Professional top-down investors may spend weeks or months researching themes including field trips, interviews, and discussions with specialists.

Acquiring the proper top-down skill set tilts toward the experiential and qualitative. Masters of macro investing have honed their skills through direct experience and familiarity with prior cycles and market movements. The same holds true for investors who focus on secular shifts. That does not mean, however, that key top-down pillars cannot be taught.

To start, you can research and study a great deal about the categories in Exhibit 1.3:

EXHIBIT 1.3 Top-Down Approach

Top-Down Approach

- Cycles, Booms & Busts

- Economics & Geopolitics

- Secular Shifts

- Industry Inflections

- **Cycles, Booms & Busts** – the ability to identify clear cyclical winners and losers, as well as out-of-favor sectors that may be on the verge of a rebound. Historical perspective and familiarity is particularly helpful here.

- **Economics & Geopolitics** – understanding the effect on stocks from Fed policy, interest rates, consumer data, unemployment levels, manufacturing data, currency exchange rates, domestic politics, and global geopolitical events

- **Secular Shifts** – companies or sectors that may be the beneficiaries or victims of anticipated changes in technology, consumer preferences, demographics, industry dynamics, or regulatory regimes

- **Industry Inflections** – sector metrics and how they move through various cycles. This also relates to commodity prices such as oil, copper, and iron ore that affect certain industries more than others.

Cycles, Booms & Busts

A keen understanding of business cycles is critical for uncovering opportunities. The recognition of familiar patterns and interrelationships helps you identify optimal entry and exit points. At a minimum, this means recognizing whether the market is early-, mid-, or late-cycle. You then invest accordingly.

Cyclical plays tend to share common qualities that you can use to your advantage. Multiples are often higher early-stage, gradually reverting to the mean, and contracting later-stage as earnings mature. This is tied to future earnings growth expectations—the higher the expected earnings growth, the higher the multiple.

In some cases, "getting the cycle right" supersedes all your bottom-up work. A stock with great financials and a strong management team might seem exciting, but it won't work if you're fighting the cycle. Even blue chips got hammered during the dot-com bubble burst in the late 1990s and the Great Recession of 2008/09.

Ideally, you want to move early in the cycle. This also applies to cyclical patterns within sectors or regions/countries. For example, coming out of the Great Recession, North American auto production was well below prior peak levels. Auto production levels had even dipped well below vehicle scrappage (see Exhibit 1.4), a clear indicator of pent-up demand. Cyclical tailwinds were blowing in support of the auto sector, which was a major contributor to the Delphi investment thesis in 2011. Of course, this same favorable cyclical breeze could also shift in the opposite direction—see Post-Mortem.

As with sectors, you can find interesting cyclical plays related to countries or regions. While the global economy has become increasingly correlated, there are clear outperformers and underperformers at any given time. Emerging markets have their own cadence vs. traditional developed markets. There may also be dramatic differences in growth and outlook between developed markets such as the U.S., Europe, and Japan.

EXHIBIT 1.4 N. American Auto Production vs. Vehicles Scrapped *(vehicles in millions)*

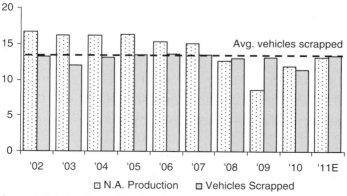

Source: IHS Automotive and Barclays Capital

Economics & Geopolitics

Reading the tea leaves on key economic and geopolitical data is yet another tool for finding ideas. This data may paint a broad brush and overshadow company-specific information. The bullish trade of the century centered on interpreting dovish monetary policy from global central banks post-Great Recession as a green light. The Fed mandate to promote full employment and control inflation led to low interest rates, creating a highly favorable environment for stocks.

Beyond interest rates, you need to understand employment data, wage statistics, inflation, GDP growth, consumer confidence, and tax policy. To some extent, they are interrelated. For example, weak wage data or underemployment would suggest continued dovish monetary policy. Accelerated inflation or wage growth, on the other hand, might signal Fed tightening ahead. Similarly, GDP growth, consumer confidence, and manufacturing output data are informative in their own right, while also providing insight on Fed (in)action. Tying all these macro data points together enables you to invest accordingly.

Domestic and global geopolitical events, such as major elections, regime changes, and military conflict, also need to be monitored closely. Global interconnectivity is a reality as are cross-border ramifications, such as trade/tariff policies, population flows, and economic alliances. The U.S. stock market is not immune to events in China, Europe, and key emerging markets, and vice versa.

In February 2016, many high-quality companies traded off materially due to deep concerns about the slowing Chinese economy. Later that year, they rebounded dramatically. Global dislocations often create compelling entry points. This is especially true for quality stocks whose fundamental thesis remains intact. The so-called Brexit vote in June 2016 also created a temporary market dislocation. Stocks traded off meaningfully across the board, only to snap back shortly thereafter.

Secular Shifts

Secular shifts create sustainable tailwinds for those stocks on the right side of the breeze. Investors are constantly on the lookout for seismic changes in technology, consumer preferences, and demographics. This extends across all industries and geographies. So, how do you identify these shifts?

A large part of the secret sauce involves keeping to the basics. As noted earlier, successful investors pay attention to what is going on in the world. They consume news voraciously, and are observant in everyday life. For example, your online shopping has increased exponentially.

You now book your travel online. When purchasing a car, you are offered a whole slew of new electronic options. Who benefits and who suffers? Simple observations like these can guide new stock ideas.

On the other hand, beware the secular buzzsaw. Look no further than Amazon and the e-commerce phenomenon, which has upended brick-and-mortar retail. It's largely a zero-sum game with big winners taking share from eventual losers.

Timing is also key. Some secular shifts may take years to play out. So while your thesis may be right, your timing may be off. What seems like a tidal wave may prove to be a mere ripple. In the interim, your stock picks may stagnate or even falter.

Even worse, the secular play may be a false positive. A company's great idea and accompanying product may attract a strong competitive response. There are countless examples of upstarts being squashed by well-capitalized fast followers.

So, back to secular winners. Early investors in digital advertising, smart phones, and social media earned outsized returns on companies such as Alphabet, Apple, and Facebook. Similarly, those who recognized the sea change in video consumption and backed Netflix reaped the benefits. Over the next decade, investors will seek to figure out the best way to play various structural shifts, among them the "sharing economy," autonomous driving, and artificial intelligence.

Industry Inflections

Some investors specialize in specific sectors. Consumer, energy, healthcare, industrials, and technology come to mind. These specialists draw upon considerable expertise, networks, and databases to identify trends and assess prospects. As with any specialization, this type of insight provides advantages vs. generalists.

For any given sector, certain data moves the corresponding stocks disproportionately to the overall market. Auto sales dictate how auto stocks perform, retail sales affect selected consumer names, and housing starts drive homebuilders. They also tend to have their own cycles, which correlate to the broader economy in varying degrees.

Ideally, you want to find sector plays with both macro/cyclical and secular tailwinds. Let's look at the U.S. cable industry for the 2010 to 2017 period. Cable typically thrives in an expansionary economy given its ties to discretionary spending and housing. It is also relatively recession-resistant given its subscription-based model and critical-needs products.

Early 2010 represented an inflection point for the cable industry as secular trends aligned with the broader macro recovery (see Exhibit 1.5). Previously, companies like Charter Communications (CHTR) and Comcast Corporation (CMCSA) were engaged in bitter hand-to-hand combat with traditional telecom companies such as AT&T (T) over new internet subscribers. Cable started to emerge as the clear winner, however, due to superior network reliability and faster download speeds at a better price. Early investors in cable rode favorable trends for several years while telecom investors underperformed.

More broadly, your industry analysis helps allocate opportunities on a portfolio basis. You can identify sectors with cyclical, macro, secular, or structural tailwinds, while avoiding those with headwinds. For example, you may see dynamic growth in certain new media or tech segments and overweight accordingly, while avoiding or even shorting the donor sectors.

EXHIBIT 1.5 Cable vs. Telco Share of Broadband Subscriber Adds

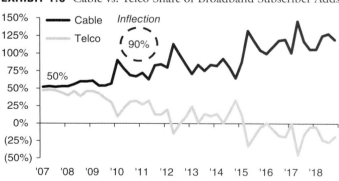

Source: Company filings

Key Takeaways

- *Idea generation takes many forms, from reading industry standards to everyday life observations to more sophisticated screening tools*

- *Bottom-up focuses on the fundamentals of individual companies, while top-down seeks opportunities based on macro or secular themes*

- *Top-down focuses on economic and geopolitical drivers, as well as cycles and secular shifts*

- *Look for stock ideas among undervalued companies, M&A situations, spin-offs, IPOs, restructurings & turnarounds, and buybacks & dividends, among others*

- *Most "cheap" stocks are cheap for a reason—the key is to find stocks that are cheap because they are misunderstood by the market*

- *An M&A-centric approach can take many forms— transformational deals, sector consolidation, natural targets, and proven acquirers*

- *Ideally, you want to find sector plays with both macro/cyclical and secular tailwinds*

Chapter Two

Step II:
Identifying the Best Ideas

Now you have a list of ideas, what's next?

The initial idea generation process outlined in Step I is designed to produce a short list of stocks for further consideration. This "short list," however, may include several dozen or more potential ideas. So, how do you analyze all these opportunities in an orderly fashion?

Pros turn to an organized process to help sift through potential investments early on and assess whether they merit further consideration. In this chapter, we provide a framework and accompanying template to help you accomplish this. Our framework centers on *investment thesis, business model, management, risks & considerations,* and *financials & valuation.*

When filtering ideas, pros tend to apply certain criteria or "bright lines," typically informed by past winners and losers. They may be based on financial parameters related to size, growth, profitability, leverage, or valuation—e.g., companies with a market cap above $1 billion, earnings growth above 10% annually, or leverage below 3x. Others may focus on specific sectors, such as consumer, industrials, or telecom, or situations, such as M&A, spin-offs, or turnarounds. You will develop your own rules of engagement over time. But, remember that successful investing requires continuous learning and adaptability. Bright lines can always be revisited.

When reviewing your initial list, certain ideas may jump off the page as potential core investments. In most cases, however, the ideas with the highest upside are not so black and white. You often need to dig deep and defy skeptics before the full merits of the stock are unearthed.

Returning to our IPO example from Step I, Delphi stood out as a stock worth further exploration. Its bankruptcy taint was still fresh, and its business revamp still unproven. This meant many investors were steering clear. A sizable valuation discount vs. peers made it even more intriguing. In Step II, we apply our framework to further scrutinize the opportunity.

Idea Review Framework

The framework in Exhibit 2.1 is designed to help you identify the best ideas in an organized and concise manner. It also provides consistency across various types of investments. As you gain familiarity with the framework and develop your own investment criteria, you will learn to quickly eliminate clear outliers and sniff out potential winners.

EXHIBIT 2.1 Idea Review Framework

Idea Review Framework
I. Investment Thesis
II. Business Overview
III. Management
IV. Risks & Considerations
V. Financials & Valuation

In Exhibits 2.2A and 2.2B, we provide an "investment write-up template" to help organize your research on potential opportunities. We use Delphi at the time of its November 2011 IPO as our case study. As such, the work below assesses whether the stock had the makings of an attractive investment at that time.

Investment write-ups are a core tool for pros. They facilitate a methodical review process and allow for efficient sharing with team members or investment committees. Each section of the template corresponds to our idea review framework above. While our template is a succinct two-pager, an investment write-up can be much longer.

In the following pages, we walk you through each section of the template. It is Microsoft Excel-based and can be customized in accordance with the sector or situation. It is also available on our website: **www.investinglikethepros.com.** While many terms in the template may be foreign to you at this point, please be patient—we explain them in more detail throughout the book.

EXHIBIT 2.2A   Investment Write-up Template

Delphi Automotive (DLPH)   November 2011

I. Investment Thesis

- **Business rationale** – best-in-class auto supplier benefiting from global auto sales cyclical recovery and secular trends of "Safe, Green & Connected," driven by regulations and consumer preferences, as well as outsized growth in China; post-bankruptcy emerged with a refocused product portfolio, best-cost manufacturing footprint, and clean balance sheet
- **Management** – deep team led by CEO Rod O'Neal, a GM/Delphi lifer who oversaw Delphi during bankruptcy where the company eliminated unprofitable businesses, uncompetitive cost structure, and burdensome liabilities; supported by active Board of Directors laser-focused on shareholder value creation
- **Growth** – expected to grow EPS at a mid-double-digit CAGR over next few years, driven by sales growth in excess of light vehicle production due to expanding content per vehicle, increasing product penetration on new vehicle platforms, and stock buybacks
- **Margins** – estimated to improve EBITDA margins from low-double-digits to mid-teens (in line with best comps) over next five years due to product mix, operating leverage, and 90% of labor in best-cost countries
- **Capital returns** – repurchased General Motors' $4.3bn equity stake pre-IPO, expecting mix of buybacks/dividends going forward as only 0.3x net leverage, no large maturities for 5 years, and $1.45bn in cash
- **M&A** – potential M&A bolt-ons in key areas, such as engineered products, to strengthen market share positions and build scale; opportunity for further portfolio pruning to revalue the base business
- **Valuation** – trades like a "production-linked" supplier at 3.5x 2013E EV/EBITDA, 5x P/E, and ~15% FCF yield, but should trade like higher-multiple "secular grower" peers given product mix, margins, and growth profile
- **Catalysts** – accelerated earnings ramp, bolt-on acquisitions, non-core divestitures, potential initiation of new buyback or dividend program, and eventual stock sale by current core shareholders

II. Business Overview

- **Company description** – vehicle components manufacturer providing electrical/electronic, powertrain, active safety, and thermal solutions to global automotive and commercial vehicle markets; 110 manufacturing facilities in 30 countries and 102K employees
- **Products & services** – electrical architecture (40% of sales, connectors, wiring assemblies, electrical centers), powertrain systems (30%, fuel handling & injection, combustion, electronic controls), electronics & safety (19%, body controls, reception, infotainment), and thermal (11%, cooling and heating systems)
- **Customers & end markets** – all 25 of the largest automotive original equipment manufacturers ("OEMs") worldwide; 21% of sales to GM, 9% Ford, 8% VW, 6% Daimler, 5% Peugeot, 4% Renault, 3% Fiat Group; its products are found in most of the top-selling vehicle models
- **Competition** – occupies #1 or #2 position in 70% of its businesses; primary competitors include: BorgWarner, Bosch, Continental, Denso, Harman, Sumitomo, and Yazaki
- **Geographic exposure** – 33% North America, 43% Europe, 16% Asia, 8% South America (as of 2010); Asia is expected to account for 50%+ of sales growth over the next five years

III. Management

- **CEO Rod O'Neal** – $30m equity; CEO since 1/2007 and COO since 1/2005; spent 40 years at GM/Delphi
  - **Track record** – oversaw Delphi restructuring at the direction of the Board and lead shareholders, which decreased product lines from 119 to 33 and business segments from 7 to 4; reduced hourly wages, increased temporary workforce, and improved operating profit from -$1.3bn to +$1.7bn
  - **Compensation structure** – tied to achieving market value thresholds as well as key financial performance metrics, i.e., EBITDA (70% weighting), FCF (20%), and sales bookings (10%)
  - **Reputation** – industry expert: "His strength is with customers, spends most of his time closing deals. Leads from the front and has surrounded himself with top talent in the sector."
- **CFO Kevin Clark** – $15m equity, CFO since 7/2011; co-founder of private equity firm, previously CFO of Fisher Scientific ('01–'06) where he helped drive 20% annual returns and grew EPS at 27% CAGR

IV. Risks & Considerations

- **Auto cycle** – underlying business tied to production levels; during last recession, peak-to-trough auto production was -43% in North America and -15% on a global basis
- **European exposure** – EU production levels forecasted to decline near-term given macro conditions and high inventory levels; offset by 25% of European sales to luxury OEMs that primarily export internationally
- **China & emerging markets** – potentially volatile economic conditions & local market competitive dynamics
- **Foreign exchange** – 65% of revenue generated outside North America, subject to variance in reported earnings given exposure to the Mexican Peso, Euro, Yuan, and British Pound
- **Raw materials** – primary production inputs are copper and resins, reliant upon ability to pass on price increases in event of sudden spikes in these commodities

EXHIBIT 2.2B Investment Write-up Template (continued)

Delphi Automotive (DLPH)

($ in millions, except per share data; shares in millions)   Fiscal Year End   Dec-31

V. Financials & Valuation

			Sector Corp Ratings	Automotive Ba2 / BB

Market Data

Share Price	52-Wk Return	% of 52-Wk High	Diluted Shares	Market Cap	Enterprise Value	Avg. Daily Volume
$22.00	NA	100%	328	$7,221	$8,501	NA

Financial Summary

	Historical			Projected		
	2009A	2010A	2011E	2012E	2013E	2014E
Sales	$11,755	$13,817	$16,039	$16,594	$18,023	$19,507
% growth	*(30.1%)*	*17.5%*	*16.1%*	*3.5%*	*8.6%*	*8.2%*
Gross Profit	$228	$2,049	$2,526	$2,671	$2,991	$3,335
% margin	*1.9%*	*14.8%*	*15.7%*	*16.1%*	*16.6%*	*17.1%*
EBITDA	$84	$1,633	$2,044	$2,157	$2,433	$2,731
% margin	*0.7%*	*11.8%*	*12.7%*	*13.0%*	*13.5%*	*14.0%*
% growth	*NM*	*NM*	*25.2%*	*5.5%*	*12.8%*	*12.2%*
D&A	$679	$421	$478	$490	$532	$575
Net Income	($866)	$631	$1,072	$1,180	$1,371	$1,577
% margin	*(7.4%)*	*4.6%*	*6.7%*	*7.1%*	*7.6%*	*8.1%*
Diluted Shares	686	686	328	324	314	304
EPS	($1.26)	$0.92	$3.27	$3.65	$4.36	$5.19
% growth	*NM*	*NM*	*255.0%*	*11.7%*	*19.7%*	*19.0%*
Cash from Ops.	($98)	$1,142	$1,356	$1,639	$1,836	$2,083
Less: Capex	(409)	(500)	(629)	(747)	(811)	(878)
Free Cash Flow	($507)	$642	$727	$892	$1,025	$1,205
% growth	*NM*	*NM*	*13.2%*	*22.8%*	*14.9%*	*17.5%*
FCF / S	($0.74)	$0.94	$2.21	$2.76	$3.26	$3.97
% growth	*NM*	*NM*	*136.7%*	*24.5%*	*18.4%*	*21.5%*

Credit Statistics

Interest Exp.	8	30	123	123	121	120
Total Debt	396	289	2,103	2,028	1,992	1,956
Cash	3,107	3,219	1,455	2,012	2,651	3,370
EBITDA / Int. Exp.	10.5x	54.4x	16.6x	17.5x	20.0x	22.7x
(EBITDA-Cpx.) / Int. Exp.	NM	37.8x	11.5x	11.5x	13.4x	15.4x
Debt / EBITDA	4.7x	0.2x	1.0x	0.9x	0.8x	0.7x
Net Debt / EBITDA	NM	(1.8x)	0.3x	0.0x	(0.3x)	(0.5x)

Valuation & Returns

EV / Sales	0.7x	0.6x	0.5x	0.5x	0.5x	0.4x
EV / EBITDA	NM	5.2x	4.2x	3.9x	3.5x	3.1x
P / E	NM	23.9x	6.7x	6.0x	5.0x	4.2x
P / FCF	NM	23.5x	9.9x	8.0x	6.7x	5.5x
FCF Yield	*NM*	*4.3%*	*10.1%*	*12.5%*	*14.8%*	*18.0%*
ROIC	*NM*	*12.6%*	*20.5%*	*22.3%*	*25.4%*	*28.8%*
Dividend Yield	-	-	-	-	-	-
Buybacks	$0	$0	$4,738	$250	$350	$450

Comparable Companies

Company	Ticker	EV / EBITDA		P / E		FCF Yield		Debt / EBITDA	EBITDA Margin	ROIC	EPS CAGR
		12E	13E	12E	13E	12E	13E				
Autoliv	ALV	4.2x	4.0x	7.9x	7.6x	9.6%	9.8%	0.6x	14%	16%	2%
BorgWarner	BWA	7.8x	6.8x	13.1x	11.0x	5.9%	7.2%	1.8x	15%	13%	17%
Harman	HAR	6.0x	5.3x	13.5x	11.9x	8.2%	8.2%	1.3x	10%	7%	17%
Magna	MGA	3.5x	3.1x	7.7x	6.5x	8.6%	10.5%	0.1x	7%	9%	15%
Tenneco	TEN	4.3x	3.8x	8.4x	7.0x	9.7%	11.3%	2.2x	8%	14%	NM
Delphi	**DLPH**	**3.9x**	**3.5x**	**6.0x**	**5.0x**	**12.5%**	**14.8%**	**1.0x**	**13%**	**21%**	**17%**
Mean		**5.1x**	**4.6x**	**10.1x**	**8.8x**	**8.4%**	**9.4%**	**1.2x**	**11%**	**12%**	**16%**

I. Investment Thesis

An investment thesis is exactly as it sounds—the core merits that support ownership of a given stock. It is the very foundation of the investment decision, justifying why you believe the stock is worth owning.

The thesis should be succinct, organized, and accessible. It also needs to be thoroughly vetted. Potential strengths must be weighed against risks, with sufficient comfort gained on critical questions. In Exhibit 2.3, we lay out the core components of an investment thesis.

EXHIBIT 2.3 Investment Thesis Components

Investment Thesis Components

- Business Rationale
- Management
- Growth
- Margins
- Capital Returns
- M&A
- Valuation
- Catalysts

Below, we flesh out the Delphi investment thesis, which corresponds to Exhibit 2.2A.

- **Business Rationale** – Why is the company worth owning? What is its special sauce? What makes it successful? Sometimes this can be fairly obvious…but usually you have to dig deeper to find whether a sustainable advantage or *moat* exists.

  - *Delphi: "best-in-class auto supplier benefiting from global auto sales cyclical recovery and secular trends of "Safe, Green and Connected," driven by regulations and consumer preferences, as well as outsized growth in China; post-bankruptcy emerged with a refocused product portfolio, best-cost manufacturing footprint, and clean balance sheet"*

- **Management** – What is management's track record in terms of operating the business and delivering value for shareholders? Is the Board playing an active role in helping shape the strategy and vision of the company?

  - *Delphi: "deep team led by CEO Rod O'Neal, a GM/Delphi lifer who oversaw Delphi during bankruptcy where the company eliminated unprofitable businesses, uncompetitive cost structure, and burdensome liabilities; supported by active Board of Directors laser-focused on shareholder value creation"*

- **Growth** – How fast is the company growing? Is it sustainable? Is the growth primarily organic or acquisition-driven, or a combination? What are the secular trends? How do growth rates compare to sector peers? Are there any financial/non-operational earnings drivers such as buybacks, refinancings, or net operating losses (NOLs)?[1]

  - *Delphi: "expected to grow EPS at a mid-double-digit CAGR over next few years, driven by sales growth in excess of light vehicle production due to expanding content per vehicle, increasing product penetration on new vehicle platforms, and stock buybacks"*

- **Margins** – How do margins compare to historical levels? What is the trajectory? Are they higher or lower than peers? If lower, is there a clear path for improvement, e.g., cost-cutting, operating leverage,[2] pricing power, product mix? If higher, does the company have cost advantages or scale efficiencies? Or, is it just a temporary benefit due to successful raw material hedges or competitor disruptions?

---

[1] *NOL carryforward* is a loss incurred in a prior period that can be used to offset future taxable income.

[2] Extent to which each dollar of incremental sales translates into incremental operating income.

- ○ *Delphi:* *"estimated to improve EBITDA margins from low-double-digits to mid-teens (in line with best comps) over next five years due to product mix, operating leverage, and 90% of labor in best-cost countries (BCCs)"*

- **Capital Returns** – Does the company have a share repurchase or dividend program in place? Is there sufficient FCF generation or balance sheet capacity to support higher buyback or dividend levels?

    - ○ *Delphi:* *"repurchased General Motors' $4.3bn equity stake pre-IPO, expecting mix of buybacks/ dividends going forward as only 0.3x net leverage, no large maturities for 5 years, and $1.45bn in cash"*

- **M&A** – What is the company's M&A track record? What is the state of the current M&A and financing environment? Are there actionable targets with motivated sellers? Are asset prices reasonable? Is the company itself a potential target? Does it have non-core assets that can be spun or sold?

    - ○ *Delphi:* *"potential M&A bolt-ons in key areas, such as engineered components, to strengthen market share positions and build scale; opportunity for further portfolio pruning to revalue the base business"*

- **Valuation** – Does the company trade at a premium or discount to peers and the market? Why? How does current valuation compare to historical levels? Is the stock cheap relative to its business quality, growth outlook, margin potential, and returns?

    - *Delphi: "trades like a 'production-linked' supplier at 3.5x 2013E EV/EBITDA, 5x P/E, and ~15% FCF yield, but should trade like higher-multiple 'secular grower' peers given product mix, margins, and growth profile"*

- **Catalysts** – Are there any near-, medium-, or long-term catalysts to drive the share price higher? Is the company likely to beat earnings estimates and/or raise guidance? Are new product launches expected to be impactful? Is there a new buyback program or dividend announcement on the horizon? Does the company intend to pursue M&A or spin off non-core units? Is an activist investor likely to enter and press for large-scale changes?

    - *Delphi: "accelerated earnings ramp, bolt-on acquisitions, non-core divestitures, potential initiation of new buyback or dividend program, and eventual stock sale by current core shareholders"*

II. Business Overview

Understanding "what the company actually does" is critical for your investment thesis. Yes, it is that simple. And yet, so few people actually understand the business behind the stocks they buy.

The next time someone pitches you a stock at a cocktail party, be sure to ask "What does the company do?" or "How does it make money?" Try any of the FAANG stocks. How do they really generate their profits? Don't be surprised if you are met with awkward silence or hemming and hawing.

So, where does the process of understanding a business begin? We recommend you start by reviewing the company's corporate website, SEC filings (10-Ks[3] and 10-Qs,[4] or S-1,[5] if applicable), and recent investor presentations.[6] Sell-side research reports are also helpful in

---

[3] Form 10-K is an annual report filed with the SEC by a public registrant that provides a comprehensive overview of the company and its prior year's performance. It is typically filed within 60 days of a company's fiscal year end. SEC filings are available on corporate websites or at www.sec.gov.

[4] Form 10-Q is a quarterly report filed with the SEC typically within 45 days of a company's fiscal quarter end.

[5] Form S-1 is the SEC registration statement for a company intending to go public and list on a U.S. stock exchange.

[6] See "Investor Relations" or "Investors" link on the company website.

getting up-to-speed quickly. Fortunately, you should have access to research through your brokerage account(s).[7]

Beyond a company description, key focus areas of our investment write-up template include products & services, customers & end markets, competition, and geographic exposure (see Exhibit 2.4).

EXHIBIT 2.4 Business Overview

Business Overview

- Company Description
- Products & Services
- Customers & End Markets
- Competition
- Geographic Exposure

Company Description

Understanding a company's core business operations is a gateway for everything that follows. The Company Description section states that Delphi is a:

---

[7]Most brokerage houses provide individual investors with access to in-house or affiliate research.

*"vehicle   components   manufacturer   providing
electrical/electronic, powertrain, active safety, and
thermal solutions to the global automotive and
commercial vehicle markets; has 110 manufacturing
facilities in 30 countries and 102k employees"*

Every public company is categorized by sector, which
refers to the industry or markets in which it operates.
Examples include consumer products, healthcare, industrials,
and technology, among others. These classifications can be
further categorized into sub-sector and geography. Sector
and geographic classifications are important for providing
key insights on growth drivers, competitive dynamics, and
risks. The market processes these classifications accordingly
in formulating a valuation.

Delphi, for example, is an industrials company in the
automotive sector, auto supplier sub-sector, and operates
on a global basis with a sizable Chinese business. While
Delphi's categorizations are straightforward, others may
be more difficult to pin down. Amazon.com comes to
mind—is it a tech company, or does it fall under retail,
logistics, or something yet to be determined?

Beyond sector, sub-sector, and geography, the brief
company description provides key information about Delphi.
First, the company supplies components to automotive

OEMs.[8] This means that sales are driven by global automotive demand with corresponding opportunities and challenges. Next, the company has a large customer base and operates in many countries, which suggests scale advantages and global reach.

Products & Services

Products and services are at the core of a company's business model. Key product categories are straightforward, e.g., auto parts, food & beverage, mobile devices, prescription drugs, and steel. They range from commodities to specialty goods. Key services include banking, consulting, distribution, lodging, and telecom.

The Products & Services section provides a listing of Delphi's key offerings:

"electrical architecture (40% of sales, connectors, wiring assemblies, electrical centers), powertrain systems (30%, fuel handling & injection, combustion, electronic controls), electronics & safety (19%, body controls, reception, infotainment), and thermal (11%, cooling and heating systems)"

---

[8]Automotive OEMs (original equipment manufacturers) refer to producers of cars and trucks, e.g., GM, Ford, and Volkswagen.

Delphi's core products and services were supported by strong secular growth dynamics. Tightening regulatory requirements were driving increased safety and fuel efficiency in automobiles. Meanwhile, consumers were demanding enhanced vehicle connectivity and infotainment. Per Step I, secular drivers promise above-market growth while helping insulate the company from market fluctuations and cyclicality.

When exploring a company's core products, we suggest visiting the corporate website to review photos and descriptions. Deeper diligence beyond Step II should involve trying out the products and services for yourself to the extent possible. Are they unique? Are they essential to their customers? Are there cheaper substitutes? Where do they fit in the underlying sector's ecosystem? These items underpin the long-term sustainability of a business.

Customers & End Markets

Customers refer to the purchasers of a company's products and services. The quantity and diversity of a company's customers are important. Some businesses serve a broad customer base while others target a specialized or niche market.

Low customer concentration typically translates into lower risk. At the same time, a sizable longstanding customer base helps provide visibility and comfort regarding future cash flows.

End markets refer to the broad underlying markets into which a company sells its products and services. End markets need to be distinguished from customers. A company may sell into the construction market, but to retailers or suppliers as opposed to homebuilders.

The Customers & End Markets section for Delphi notes that the company sells its products to:

> *"all 25 of the largest automotive original equipment manufacturers ("OEMs") worldwide; 21% of sales to GM, 9% Ford, 8% VW, 6% Daimler, 5% Peugeot, 4% Renault, 3% Fiat Group; its products are found in most of the top-selling vehicle models"*

Delphi greatly diversified its customer base over the years after being over 75% dependent on GM just a decade prior. At the IPO, GM was the only customer representing more than 10% of sales. Furthermore, Delphi's products were used in 17 of the 20 best-selling vehicle models in the U.S., 65% of the leading models in China, and all the top models in Europe. While this diversification was helpful in the event any one customer, model, or region suffered a setback, the emerging markets exposure carried higher volatility.

Competition

The number of players in a given industry and the nature of their interaction are critical to the success of any enterprise. Competitors may range from none (monopoly), to a select few (oligopoly), to as many as dozens or more companies offering similar products and services.

Usually, the fewer the competitors, the better. This relationship, however, is not foolproof. One or two bad actors can ruin the competitive environment. Similarly, even industries with multiple players can be attractive, depending on their behavior.

The Competition section for Delphi states that the company:

"occupies #1 or #2 position in 70% of its businesses; primary competitors include: BorgWarner, Bosch, Continental, Denso, Harman, Sumitomo, and Yazaki"

The "New Delphi" strategically reconfigured its portfolio to focus on secular growth categories where it had leadership positions and was set up to win. This was a sharp departure from the "Old Delphi" which tried to provide everything to everyone. The end result was a reduction of 119 product lines to 33.

This meant that Delphi had started to differentiate itself from the broader peer group. It was migrating towards the higher-end specialty supplier category of roughly a half dozen truly global competitors. While even this sub-category was fiercely competitive, Delphi had several advantages vs. peers.

From a competitive perspective, Delphi's strategic global footprint and low-cost base afforded service, quality, and price advantages. The company also housed a broad base of products spec'd into existing and new car platforms, which enhanced customer stickiness. Moreover, the company's revamped, engineering-based culture was delivering next generation products.

The strong alignment between the company's management team led by Rod O'Neal and the active Board was also a key differentiator. Together, they fostered a rigorous focus on value creation that permeated throughout the company. This was demonstrated by continuous cost improvement, efficient allocation of capital, and joint operational and financial fluency.

Geographic Exposure

Companies that are based in, and sell to, different regions may differ substantially in terms of key business drivers and characteristics. There tend to be fundamentally different growth rates, competitive dynamics, path(s)-to-market, cost structures, and opportunities/risks.

A U.S.-centered business, for example, will likely perform differently than one with extensive global operations. Currencies also play a role in financial performance. As a result, otherwise similar companies from a business perspective might have meaningfully different financial performance and valuations due to footprint.

The Geographic Exposure section for Delphi notes that the company is:

"33% North America, 43% Europe, 16% Asia, 8% South America (as of 2010); Asia is expected to account for 50%+ of sales growth over the next five years"

Delphi's broad geographic mix afforded both opportunity and risk. Its North American foothold provided a stable base in the world's most reliable market. Asia, and particularly China, held out the promise of outsized returns in the world's largest and fastest-growing market. Meanwhile, Europe was Delphi's greatest contributor to sales, but was mature and faced near-term headwinds with potential auto production declines. We explore the outlook and implications for each of these unique markets in Step III.

III. Management

Strong CEOs have a deep understanding of, and focus on, shareholder value. They are adept at formulating and executing a sound strategy that is directly linked to driving cash flow, returns, and per share metrics. The top CEOs tend to be good communicators with investors, effective at articulating their strategy and the investment opportunity in their stock. Of course, talk is just talk. Their vision needs to be supported by performance. The same holds true for other key constituents who are integral to the company's strategy, e.g., CFO, COO, or Board members.

Investors often debate whether to bet on the horse or the jockey. Many are firm believers in the horse—the implication being that even the best CEO cannot fix a fundamentally flawed company. Or, that a great business can run itself. But, why debate? Why not have both—a compelling business with a great CEO and team?

Few would disagree that management is a critical success driver regardless of the business. At a minimum, quality companies require talented leaders to keep them on track. More realistically, they are challenged every day to elevate performance and stay a step ahead of the competition. On the other end of the spectrum, troubled companies require skilled management to navigate through difficult times and right the ship.

Assessment of company management is a fundamental part of due diligence. For many investors, a strong CEO is a gating item. Certain CEOs have an almost cult-like following among investors. Exhibit 2.5 outlines a basic framework for assessing CEO or management team quality.

EXHIBIT 2.5 Management Assessment

Management Assessment
■ Track Record
■ Compensation Structure
■ Reputation

Track Record

Perhaps the best indicator of CEO quality is track record, most notably shareholder returns. Examine share price performance under the CEO's leadership, including vs. peers and indices such as the S&P 500. You should also study sales and earnings growth, both on an absolute and relative basis.

Of course, prior track record can be misleading and "past performance is not always an indicator of future success." It may be difficult to separate favorable sector trends from CEO performance or just blind luck. However, a consistent track record of outperforming peers at multiple companies and through various cycles is compelling.

One such CEO is legendary value creator John Malone. As head of Tele-Communications (TCI) from 1973 through its acquisition by AT&T in 1999, Malone drove the share price from a split-adjusted sub-$0.25 to over $65. This represented a 30% annualized return vs. 14% for the S&P 500 over the same period. Malone has since been involved in dozens of other publicly-traded companies that have generated above-market returns.

At Delphi, Rod O'Neal became President and COO in January 2005 and was promoted to CEO in January 2007. Handed the reins of a bankrupt company with a structurally uncompetitive cost structure, O'Neal led a team that implemented a bold action plan. Delphi dramatically reduced the number of product lines, eliminated burdensome union agreements, migrated 91% of the hourly workforce to BCCs, and divested numerous loss-making units.

O'Neal's key lieutenant, CFO Kevin Clark, had a demonstrated track record dating back to his days at Fisher Scientific. He had proven himself particularly adept at cost discipline, capital allocation, and M&A. Further, Chairman Jack Krol came to Delphi with a 30-year track record of success at DuPont, one of the world's largest and most sophisticated global industrial companies.

Exhibit 2.6 shows the impact of the team's actions:

EXHIBIT 2.6 Delphi Transformation

Delphi Transformation			
	2005	2010	% Difference
Business Metrics			
Product Lines	119	33	(72%)
Business Segments	7	4	(43%)
Headcount	200K	102K	(49%)
UAW Employment	23K	-	(100%)
% Labor in Best-Cost Countries	30%	91%	61%
Flexible Workforce	8%	30%	22%
Pension & OPEB Liability	$9.2bn	$0.7bn	(92%)
SG&A Spend	$1.6bn	$0.9bn	(44%)
Capex	$1.2bn	$0.5bn	(58%)
Sales Mix (% of total)			
Geographic Mix			
North America	68%	33%	(35%)
Europe	25%	43%	18%
Asia Pacific	2%	16%	14%
South America	5%	8%	3%
Customer Mix			
General Motors	48%	21%	(27%)
Ford	5%	9%	4%
Volkswagen	3%	8%	5%

Compensation Structure

Executive stock ownership and compensation structure are also informative. Equity incentives tied to ambitious performance targets or share price hurdles tend to signal conviction.

CEO Rod O'Neal and CFO Kevin Clark were both highly incentivized to drive value for Delphi's shareholders. As part of the company's incentive plan designed by the Board in collaboration with Silver Point and Elliott (dubbed the "Value Creation Plan"), O'Neal and Clark were awarded 1.35 million and 675K shares of stock, respectively. This equated to roughly $30 million and $15 million, respectively, at the $22 IPO price, thereby creating strong alignment with shareholders. Furthermore, annual compensation going forward was tied to key financial hurdles weighted towards EBITDA (70%), FCF (20%), and sales bookings (10%).

Reputation

While CEO reputation may be subjective, some initial digging can be quite revealing. As pros get more serious about a stock opportunity, they consult with industry leaders, competitors, and sell-side research analysts. Of course, anecdotal evidence needs to be cross-checked with factual support and track record.

Beyond operational excellence and shareholder value creation, you need to get comfortable with management's moral compass and trustworthiness. In accordance with the saying "a fish rots from the head down," most frauds and accounting irregularities can be traced back to senior management. By gaining confidence in the team's ethics early on, you help remove a major risk.

Over the course of his 40+ years at Delphi and its GM predecessor, O'Neal earned a strong reputation for leadership and integrity both inside and outside the company. During bankruptcy, O'Neal oversaw a high-impact action plan, which the Board and controlling shareholders helped shape and deliver. Successful execution also required inspiring the company's rank and file to spring to action despite the pains and distractions of bankruptcy.

IV. Risks & Considerations

Risk assessment refers to identifying and quantifying factors that could derail your investment thesis. You need to think long and hard about what can go wrong. These pitfalls may range from broad macro hazards to highly detailed company- or sector-specific issues. Some risks are more meaningful, some can be mitigated, and some are out of the company's control.

Of course, any investment decision carries risk. The key is to accurately identify and process it upfront. Sizable risk may represent sizable opportunity. There can be substantial upside in troubled companies through cyclical rebound, restructuring, deleveraging, new strategy, or management upgrade. Similarly, a low-risk situation may present limited prospects for attractive returns.

Regardless, the "risk/reward" relationship needs to be intact—higher risk needs to be compensated with higher returns. By quantifying the risks associated with a given stock, you can compare them to the upside potential and make an informed decision. This is a critical part of establishing your price target (PT) for a given stock (see Step IV).

Public companies provide investors some help in this regard. They are required to list and discuss the predominant risks facing the business in their 10-K filings under a section entitled "Risk Factors." While these risk factors provide helpful guidelines, it is imperative to do your own work and form your own opinions on the most serious risks.

Some companies, such as consumer staples, are relatively stable with risks tied to the overall economy or vendor issues. Others, such as auto or steel companies, are more cyclical with risks linked to underlying end markets, commodities, and currencies. Still others may face fundamental risks of obsolescence or substitution, such as brick-and-mortar retail.

For Delphi, we provide a summary overview of key risks in Exhibit 2.2A, as well as a comprehensive assessment in Step III. Given the company's 2009 emergence from bankruptcy and the auto sector's dramatic decline during the Great Recession, the cyclical nature of global auto production was the primary risk. Investor sentiment was truly challenging at the time.

The company's heavy European exposure also required scrutiny given the weak near-term outlook. Meanwhile, China's exciting growth story masked potential volatility and geopolitical uncertainty. Underlying the European and Chinese exposure was foreign currency risk with 65% of sales denominated in currencies other than the U.S. Dollar (USD). Volatility in foreign currency exchange (FX) rates could potentially lower reported USD earnings or negatively impact price competitiveness.

Lastly, raw material spikes posed a potential threat to margins, particularly large fluctuations in the price of copper and resin products. While Delphi had a track record of passing through cost increases to customers, there were no guarantees going forward. At the same time, the company's growing emerging markets exposure provided a natural hedge against raw material price spikes. Commodity prices and emerging markets performance tend to be highly correlated.

V. Financials & Valuation

At this point, you have a basic understanding of the business and formulated a thesis. Now it is time to explore the company's financials and valuation. For financials, pay particular attention to key trends and opportunities for improvement. For valuation, be on high alert for unwarranted discounts (or premiums) vs. peers.

In Exhibit 2.7, we outline key focus areas for your initial review. The headings correspond to the second page of our investment write-up template (see Exhibit 2.2B).

EXHIBIT 2.7 Financials & Valuation

Financials & Valuation
■ Market Data
■ Financial Summary
■ Credit Statistics
■ Valuation & Returns
■ Comparable Companies

Market Data

The Market Data section of our template displays basic stock information, including share price, 52-week return,[9] percentage of 52-week high, share count, and average daily volume (ADV). We also show market cap, net debt, and enterprise value.

Market Cap (or Equity Value) is the value ascribed to a company's equity by the stock market. It is simply the company's current share price multiplied by its *diluted shares* (see Exhibit 2.8).[10]

EXHIBIT 2.8 Calculation of Market Cap

Enterprise Value is the sum of all ownership interests in a company, specifically claims on assets from both debt and equity holders. In other words, the sum of the equity, debt, and their equivalents including preferred stock and noncontrolling interest.[11] Cash and equivalents are then subtracted as an offset to debt (see Exhibit 2.9).

---

[9] Year-to-date (YTD) data is also commonly used.

[10] Fully diluted shares are calculated as the sum of a company's basic shares plus "in-the-money" stock options, warrants, and convertible securities.

[11] Portion of stock in a company subsidiary that is not owned by the parent corporation.

EXHIBIT 2.9 Calculation of Enterprise Value

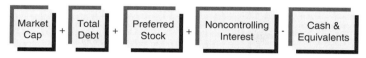

While by no means conclusive, market cap and enterprise value can be quite informative. Size provides clues about scale, competitive position, purchasing power, and growth prospects. Trading volume tells you about a stock's liquidity. This helps you gauge the depth of the market for the stock, including how many days are needed to exit the position.

Taken together, market cap and liquidity affect the nature and breadth of a company's shareholder base, and potentially its valuation. For example, companies above a certain size and liquidity may be eligible for inclusion in key equity indices or ETFs, and therefore attract a broader group of investors. Furthermore, the stock's 52-week or YTD return and % of 52-week high help inform whether the opportunity has already been discovered by the market.

Per Exhibit 2.2B, Delphi's IPO on November 16, 2011 priced at $22 per share. The company had 328 million shares, equating to a $7.2 billion market cap. Adding roughly $820 million of net debt and $462 million of noncontrolling interest resulted in an enterprise value of $8.5 billion.

Financial Summary

The Financial Summary section displays key historical and projected financial data. In Exhibit 2.2B, we show sales, gross profit, EBITDA, net income, and free cash flow. We also show per share metrics, i.e., EPS and FCF/S. A quick analysis of growth rates, profitability, and FCF generation can tell you a great deal about the health of a company and its prospects.

For growth rates, investors examine both historical and projected top and bottom line performance, paying close attention to accelerating or decelerating trends. Sell-side consensus estimates[12] for the future two-to-three-year period provide initial perspective. Presumably these numbers are somewhat guided by management.

Profitability measures a company's ability to convert sales into profit, expressed as margins. Profit margins employ a measure of earnings in the numerator, such as gross profit, EBITDA, or net income, and sales in the denominator. Higher growth rates and profit margins typically translate into higher valuations.

---

[12] Average or median of the research analysts covering a particular stock.

Free cash flow generation is a critical indicator of a company's financial health. It measures the actual cash produced by a company, factoring in capital expenditures (capex)[13] and net working capital (NWC).[14] There are numerous ways to calculate FCF with the most basic formula being cash flow from operations[15] *less* capex (see Exhibit 2.10). It can also be calculated as net income *plus* depreciation & amortization (D&A)[16] *less* capex *less* increases in NWC. A third option is to start with EBITDA and then subtract taxes, interest expense, capex, and increases in NWC.

Healthy FCF generation provides flexibility for various capital allocation options. It is "free" to invest in organic growth projects, fund M&A, return capital to shareholders, repay debt, or simply keep as dry powder. As such, it is closely watched by investors.

---

[13]Capex are the funds that a company uses to purchase, improve, expand, or replace PP&E (see Chapter 3 for more details).

[14]NWC refers to the amount of cash a company requires to fund its operations on a short-term basis (see Chapter 3 for more details).

[15]Refers to the cash generated by a company during a specific time period before considering capex, as shown on the *cash flow statement*.

[16]Depreciation is a non-cash expense that approximates the reduction of the book value of a company's PP&E over an estimated useful life and reduces reported earnings. Amortization is also a non-cash expense that reduces the value of a company's definite life intangible assets and lowers reported earnings.

EXHIBIT 2.10 Methods for Calculating Free Cash Flow

($ in millions)

FCF Calculation						
Option 1		**Option 2**		**Option 3**	
Cash Flow from Operations	$1,000	Net Income	$650	EBITDA	$1,565
Less: Capex	(500)	Plus: D&A	450	Less: Taxes	(315)
		Less: Capex	(500)	Less: Interest Expense	(150)
		Less: Inc. in NWC	(100)	Less: Capex	(500)
				Less: Inc. in NWC	(100)
Free Cash Flow	**$500**	**Free Cash Flow**	**$500**	**Free Cash Flow**	**$500**

As you review the company's financials, start jotting down key questions based on your observations. These questions will be explored further in Step III, where you perform more detailed due diligence and craft a full financial model.

For example, based on Exhibit 2.2B, key questions for Delphi at this stage might include:

- What drove the nearly 18% sales growth from 2009 to 2010, after a dramatic decline in the prior year?

- Why did gross margins expand substantially from 2009 to 2010?

- Why did diluted shares decline so dramatically from 2009 to 2011?

- Going forward, why are gross profit and EBITDA margins expected to continue to increase?

- Is it realistic for EPS to increase more than 50% by 2014E?

- Why does net income meaningfully exceed FCF going forward?

Credit Statistics

The Credit Statistics section provides a snapshot of the company's balance sheet and credit quality. While the overall debt amount is important, leverage and coverage ratios are more telling. Even ratio analysis, however, must be supplemented by more qualitative factors, such as sector, cycle, and track record.

Acceptable leverage and coverage levels vary by sector and business model. A company with a highly visible and reliable cash flow stream is better positioned to support higher leverage levels. Think cable or subscription-based software companies. Ditto for one with a large, liquid asset base.[17] A cyclical business or one with high customer concentration, on the other hand, should maintain a more conservative balance sheet.

For certain investors, credit quality is a gating item. Companies with leverage above, or coverage below, a certain level may not survive an initial screen despite other favorable business characteristics. Trends are also critical. Declining leverage and increasing coverage are signs of improving financial health.

---

[17]Lenders tend to favor companies with substantial assets that can be readily liquidated to repay debt during periods of distress.

Leverage refers to a company's debt level, typically measured as a multiple of EBITDA, e.g., debt-to-EBITDA. Investors also look at net debt-to-EBITDA, which adjusts for cash on the company's balance sheet (see Exhibit 2.11). A company's leverage reveals a great deal about financial policy, risk profile, and capacity for growth.

As a general rule, the higher a company's leverage, the higher its risk of financial distress. This is due to the burden associated with greater interest expense and principal repayments. As noted earlier, however, certain businesses are better able to support higher leverage.

Delphi's 2011E debt/EBITDA of 1x and 0.3x on a net basis was strong by any measure.

EXHIBIT 2.11 Leverage Ratios

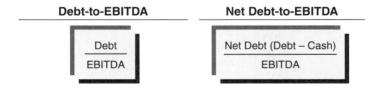

Debt-to-EBITDA	Net Debt-to-EBITDA
$\dfrac{\text{Debt}}{\text{EBITDA}}$	$\dfrac{\text{Net Debt (Debt} - \text{Cash)}}{\text{EBITDA}}$

Coverage is a broad term that refers to a company's ability to meet ("cover") its interest expense obligations. Coverage ratios comprise an operating cash flow statistic in the numerator and interest expense in the denominator, e.g., EBITDA-to-interest expense. (EBITDA *less* capex)-to-interest expense, which nets out the company's capital expenditures, can be even more informative for credit quality (see Exhibit 2.12).

Intuitively, the higher the coverage ratio, the better positioned the company is to meet its debt obligations. Like its leverage level, Delphi's 2011E EBITDA-to-interest expense of 16.6x was very healthy.

EXHIBIT 2.12 Coverage Ratios

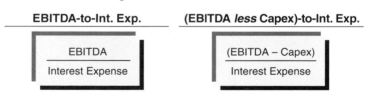

Independent credit rating agencies, including Moody's Investors Service (Moody's), Standard & Poor's (S&P), and Fitch Ratings (Fitch), provide formal assessments of corporate credit profiles. The higher the rating, the higher the deemed credit quality.[18]

---

[18] Moody's uses an alphanumeric scale, while S&P and Fitch use an alphabetic system combined with pluses (+) and minuses (-) to rate creditworthiness.

Valuation & Returns

The Valuation & Returns section displays various metrics, including EV/EBITDA, P/E, FCF yield, and ROIC. We also measure capital returns, including dividend yield and buybacks. Depending on the company or sector, certain valuation metrics may be more relevant than others.

The ability to assess value is paramount for stock picking. Based on your initial work, you may find that a company's share price is fairly valued. This is often the case. Things get a lot more interesting, however, when you spot a major disconnect between a company's share price and what you think it's actually worth.

Upfront, you perform a "quick-and-dirty" valuation to get a sense of whether the opportunity is worth pursuing. If the situation looks compelling, a thorough valuation analysis will be needed (see Step IV).

Valuation

Trading multiples form the core of valuation. A company's multiple should reflect its quality, performance, and outlook. Higher growth rates, superior margins, and lower leverage vs. peers should result in a higher multiple. A departure from this relationship may represent opportunity.

Enterprise Value-to-EBITDA (EV/EBITDA) serves as a valuation standard across most sectors (see Exhibit 2.13). This broad application stems from the fact that it is independent of capital structure and taxes. Therefore, two similar companies with different debt levels should still have relatively similar EV/EBITDA multiples.[19] EV/EBITDA is also more relevant for companies with little or no net income. Examples include highly leveraged, deeply cyclical, and early-stage companies.

EV/EBITDA also normalizes for distortions that may arise from D&A differences among companies. One company may have spent heavily on new equipment in recent years, resulting in elevated D&A, while another company may have deferred its capital spending.

Delphi's 2013E EV/EBITDA was 3.5x, representing a 1.1x discount to the broader peer set. Was this discrepancy due to Delphi's bankruptcy and long absence from the public market? Or did the market see more fundamental issues?

EXHIBIT 2.13 EV/EBITDA

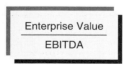

---

[19] Companies with very high debt levels, however, typically serve as exceptions due to concerns over financial distress.

Price-to-Earnings (P/E) is the most widely recognized trading multiple by Main Street (see Exhibit 2.14). P/E can be viewed as a measure of how much investors are willing to pay for a dollar of a company's earnings. Companies with higher P/Es vs. peers tend to have higher growth expectations.

P/E is particularly relevant for mature companies with a demonstrated ability to consistently grow EPS. It is less helpful for companies with little or no earnings given the denominator is *de minimis* or even negative.

P/E is also less relevant for comparing companies with different capital structures. EPS is burdened with interest expense and, therefore, influenced by debt load. So, two companies with similar sales and EBITDA margins can have substantially different P/Es due to differences in leverage.

Like Delphi's EV/EBITDA multiple, its 2013E P/E of 5x was well below that of peers with similar growth, margin, and leverage profiles. The broader group was trading at nearly 9x. Did Delphi deserve to be trading at such a large discount?

EXHIBIT 2.14 P/E

Price-to-Free Cash Flow (P/FCF per share) is calculated as current share price divided by FCF/S. In this sense, it is like P/E, but with FCF/S substituting for EPS.

Its inverse, **FCF/S-to-Share Price (FCF Yield)**, measures a company's cash flow generation as a percentage of its market cap. "FCF yield" represents cash return on equity value, as well as how much cash is theoretically available to return to shareholders (see Exhibit 2.15).

Many pros deem FCF as the most appropriate basis for valuation. Metrics such as EBITDA and EPS can be massaged, so this line of thinking goes, but "cash is king." A company can't spend EBITDA, but it can spend cash.

Delphi's 2013E FCF yield of roughly 15% vs. peers at 9.4% looked highly compelling, especially given its strong FCF/S growth profile.

EXHIBIT 2.15 P/FCF and FCF Yield

Additional multiples are sector-specific, e.g., financials, natural resources, real estate, and cable/telecom. As shown in Exhibit 2.16, these multiples feature a measure of market value in the numerator and an operating metric in the denominator.

EXHIBIT 2.16 Selected Sector-Specific Valuation Multiples

Valuation Multiples	Sector
Enterprise Value /	
EBITDA + Rent (EBITDAR)	▪ Casinos ▪ Restaurants ▪ Retail
EBITDA + Depletion & Exploration (EBITDAX)	▪ Natural Resources ▪ Oil & Gas
Reserves	▪ Natural Resources ▪ Oil & Gas
Subscriber	▪ Cable ▪ Telecom
Equity Value (Price) / per share metrics	
Book Value	▪ Financials ▪ Homebuilders
Cash Available for Distribution	▪ Real Estate
Discretionary Cash Flow	▪ Natural Resources
Funds from Operations (FFO)	▪ Real Estate
Net Asset Value (NAV)	▪ Financials ▪ Real Estate

Returns

Return on invested capital (ROIC) measures a company's ability to provide earnings (or returns) to its capital providers. As shown in Exhibit 2.17, ROIC is typically defined as tax-effected EBIT divided by a measure of invested capital. The most prevalent ways to calculate invested capital are working capital *plus* net PP&E *plus* other operating assets, or net debt *plus* equity.

Investors tend to reward companies whose return metrics consistently exceed their cost of capital.[20] These excess returns accrue to equity holders.

Delphi's ROIC was 20.5%, a healthy number on both an absolute basis and vs. peers, greatly exceeding its estimated 10% cost of capital. As noted in Step I, a high ROIC combined with a low valuation is a common screen.

EXHIBIT 2.17 ROIC

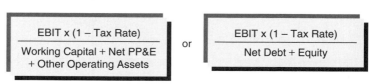

---

[20] See Chapter 4 for detailed discussion of the weighted average cost of capital (WACC).

Dividend yield measures the annual dividend per share paid by a company to its shareholders, expressed as a percentage of current share price (see Exhibit 2.18). A company with a $20 share price that pays an annual dividend of $0.50 per share has a dividend yield of 2.5%.

While dividend payers are prized by many investors for their direct return of capital, others eschew them due to tax inefficiency or perceived lack of growth. Delphi launched its IPO without a dividend. This is typical for newly listed companies so as not to detract from the growth story.

By early 2013, however, circumstances changed. Delphi's strong cash generation, confidence in the business, commitment to capital return, and desire to broaden its investor base prompted the initiation of a quarterly dividend. The yield was roughly 1.7% at the time.

EXHIBIT 2.18 Dividend Yield

$$\frac{\text{Most Recent Quarterly Dividend Per Share} \times 4}{\text{Current Share Price}}$$

Comparable Companies

The Comparable Companies ("comps") section displays a summary output for the company's closest public peers. At this stage, it should be noted that this is a preliminary comp set. By Step IV, deeper due diligence produces a more refined and segmented comps analysis.

As shown in Exhibit 2.2, key peer data includes valuation multiples, leverage ratios, EBITDA margins, ROIC, and EPS growth rates. Comps is perhaps the most common valuation tool as it provides a real-time benchmark.

The foundation for comps is built upon the premise that similar companies provide a natural reference point for benchmarking valuation. This is intuitive given they share key business and financial characteristics, performance drivers, and risks.

A quick review of the comps table in Exhibit 2.2B is revealing. Despite having roughly twice the EBITDA margins and ROIC as Magna (MGA), Delphi traded at a discount on a P/E basis. This discrepancy was exacerbated by Delphi's sector-high FCF yield. Further, while the company was reinventing itself along three core secular growth themes, the majority of MGA's business was production-driven.

Meanwhile, best-in-class peer BorgWarner (BWA), whose business was centered on powertrain, traded at more than twice the P/E and under half the FCF yield of Delphi.

This is despite the fact that Delphi had more margin upside and a better return profile. Clearly, BorgWarner was getting more credit than Delphi for its secular growth story.

Hence, based on our initial review, Delphi appeared to be mispriced vs. peers—a best-in-class premium supplier that was not yet getting credit for its secular potential. We further explore the discrepancies between Delphi and its peers in Step IV, where we show you how to benchmark peer companies and perform deeper valuation work.

Preliminary Assessment

Overall, our high level review of Delphi produced key insights. During and post-bankruptcy, the lead shareholders and Board worked effectively with management to implement numerous initiatives to cut costs and align with key secular themes. This produced a revamped business with a markedly improved product suite. We also identified potential catalysts for driving a revaluation, including operational improvements, M&A, and capital returns. We then flagged key risks related to the auto cycle, geographic exposure, and foreign currencies.

On the financial side, we saw momentum in Delphi's top and bottom lines. Valuation was compelling—the stock looked cheap vs. secular grower auto supply peers on the basis of all relevant metrics—EV/EBITDA, P/E, and FCF yield.

How real was this opportunity to get secular growth at a cyclical price? The valuation disparities between Delphi and the peer group suggested that the company was either destined to fail in its reinvention OR massively undervalued.

The work thus far suggested the latter was true. The market was seemingly still distracted by the Old Delphi and its bankruptcy stigma. Many large mutual funds were badly burned from losses on the Old Delphi and reluctant to revisit the investment with fresh eyes. Astute investors, however, were focused on the opportunity at the massively transformed New Delphi. But, more work was needed in Steps III and IV ...

Key Takeaways

- *Experienced investors employ an organized process to evaluate potential investments upfront*

- *As you develop your own investment criteria, you will be able to quickly eliminate clear outliers and home in on potential winners*

- *An investment thesis consists of core merits that support ownership of a given stock*

- *Your initial review needs to provide comfort that you want to put money behind the business*

- *Perhaps the best indicator of CEO track record is prior shareholder returns*

- *Higher risk doesn't necessarily preclude buying a stock, it just needs to be compensated with higher returns*

- *Ideally, your upfront work enables you to flag potential disconnects between a company's valuation vs. peers*

Chapter Three

Step III: Business & Financial Due Diligence

Time to take a deeper dive on your best ideas

It's now time to perform detailed business and financial due diligence. Many of the diligence items outlined below were researched at a high level in Step II. You gained initial comfort to justify additional work. Now, you are set to take a much deeper dive.

For business diligence, you are trying to figure out the quality of the company's operating model. Is it a sustainable business with a strong moat? Alternatively, has it been struggling but you see a path to redemption? Much of this analysis is qualitative, requiring sound judgment and insight. Experience and familiarity with specific business models and sectors is particularly helpful. We will help you develop the skills to quickly dissect a business.

For financial diligence, you must examine the company's core financial statements to determine where it has been and where it is going. A large portion of this analysis is making observations about key financial items and seeking defensible answers. Why are sales going up or down? Why are margins expanding or contracting? Getting answers to the "why's" is critical.

Your overall diligence should go beyond simply identifying companies with high-quality fundamentals. Embrace the flexibility and creativity needed to unearth less obvious opportunities, including underperformers with potential for substantial improvement. The latter requires high conviction gained through deep and thorough research.

But don't get overwhelmed by the due diligence process—we have created a concise framework to guide your work. Our framework takes the form of two five-question checklists, one for business diligence and one for financial. These checklists will help you organize and track your diligence process. Once completed, you will be in good shape to move forward or reject the given opportunity.

Business Due Diligence

Business due diligence centers on determining whether a company is high-quality, or can become high-quality. Beyond understanding the core business, you need to focus on its competitive position and place in the value chain. How resilient is the business model and can you gain comfort on key risks? Paramount here is whether the business solves an important problem and has long-term staying power. This deeper analysis builds on the foundation laid in Step II.

Our framework in Exhibit 3.1 is designed to help you assess whether a business is worth putting money behind. Your ability to obtain satisfactory answers to the five key questions below is critical. If the answers to these questions leave you uncomfortable, then the stock is probably not right for your portfolio. However, with each stock analyzed, you learn and improve your investment acumen.

EXHIBIT 3.1 Business Due Diligence Checklist

Business Due Diligence Checklist

I. What does the company do?

II. How does it make money?

III. What is its moat & competitive position?

IV. How strong are customer & supplier relationships?

V. What are key risks to the business?

I. What does the company do?

To paraphrase some of the world's top investors, unless you can quickly describe what a company does in plain English, then the stock is probably not for you. Peter Lynch famously explained: "The simpler it is, the better I like it."

While highly complex businesses may present opportunity, they often present increased risk. There are typically more potential unknowns and uncertainties to consider, and more things can go wrong. Common sense dictates that if you don't understand a business, then you shouldn't invest in it. On the other hand, as your skill set expands, your comfort level with complexity will expand alongside. Sizable reward may await those who solve what perplexes others.

Study as much company- and sector-specific material as possible to learn the in-depth "story." Per Step II, key sources include the Annual Report, SEC filings, investor presentations, and sell-side research reports. In Step III, next level research involves combing through prior earnings releases, call transcripts, and industry journals. You should also read the company's letter to shareholders in its Annual Report, which can be revealing in terms of corporate culture and identity. Ideally, sample the product and ask around for other people's opinions. Pros talk to industry experts and executives for insight.

Beyond the basic business model, you seek insights into why the company is worth backing. Is it a secular grower, with demand for its products and services accelerating? Is it gaining market share? Are there meaningful growth or profitability initiatives in place?

Returning to Delphi, initial work in Step II revealed key information about the business, but far from enough to fully appreciate the opportunity. We know that the company manufactures critical components for OEMs, such as General Motors, Ford, and Volkswagen. And we know that their products enable customers to meet increasing driver safety requirements, tighter fuel economy and emission standards, and evolving consumer preferences. Now, in Step III, we explore the core product offering in more detail as well as the staying power of the secular drivers.

As highlighted in the investment write-up in Exhibit 2.2, Delphi was structured around four primary business units, each providing products for distinct vehicle solutions:

- **Electrical/Electronic Architecture** (40% of sales) – provides complete design of a vehicle's electrical architecture, including connectors, wiring assemblies & harnesses, electrical centers, and hybrid power distribution systems

- **Powertrain Systems** (30% of sales) – integrates engine management systems including fuel handling & injection, combustion, and electronic controls

- **Electronics & Safety** (19% of sales) – provides critical components, systems, and software for passenger safety & security, infotainment, and vehicle operation, including body controls, reception & navigation systems, and displays

- **Thermal Systems** (11% of sales) – provides heating, ventilation & air conditioning (HVAC) systems, such as compressors, condensers, radiators, and cooling/heat exchangers

For each of its core business units, Delphi was committed to superior quality and delivery, competitive pricing, and flawless new product launches. It was also positioning its portfolio at the forefront of secular mega-trends tied to "Safe, Green and Connected." Over time, new product options related to these themes were poised to become standardized features, resulting in penetration gains.

- **Safe** – technologies intended to proactively reduce the risk of a crash occurring, as well as passenger protection in the event of a crash
  - Examples: lane departure warning systems, blind spot detection, and collision avoidance

- **Green** – technologies designed to help reduce emissions, increase fuel economy, and minimize the environmental impact of vehicles
  - Examples: products supporting hybrid and electric vehicles, as well as those that improve fuel economy and emissions, e.g., fuel injection systems

- **Connected** – technology content focused on increasing personalization, entertainment, and convenience while driving
  - Examples: integrated mobile voice & data, embedded global positioning systems (GPS), and infotainment

It should be noted that many early potential investors were skeptical of Delphi's ability to transform itself into a technology leader given its legacy. But, management and the Board were highly focused on aligning with consumer demand and regulatory tailwinds. This positioned Delphi to realize above-market growth for years to come.

II. How does it make money?

So you know what the company does. But, how does it make money? Profits are a function of sales and costs. There are four ways for a company to increase profits: increase volume, raise price, lower variable unit costs, and reduce fixed overhead.[1] The first two relate to sales, the last two relate to costs.

For most companies, two or three key business drivers truly impact performance. These are highlighted in earnings releases and investor presentations, and closely tracked by the research and investor communities. Gauging business performance and outlook relies upon understanding key dynamics for these drivers.

Sales growth drivers for both volume and price vary by sector. For a cable company, this means number of subscribers *times* monthly average revenue per user (ARPU). Subscriber count relies upon penetration of products such as video and high speed internet, while ARPU is driven by product pricing and bundling. For homebuilders, the sales growth formula is based on number of homes sold *times* average sales price (ASP). Home volumes and

---

[1] *Variable* costs change depending on the volume of goods produced and include items such as materials, direct labor, transportation, and utilities. *Fixed* costs remain more or less constant regardless of volume and include items such as lease expense, advertising and marketing, insurance, corporate overhead, and administrative salaries.

prices rely upon the strength of the housing market, which feeds from employment, wages, consumer confidence, demographic trends, lending standards, and interest rates. Ideally, you want to be aligned with secular or cyclical tailwinds that drive growth.

Cost is a function of how much expense is related to producing each unit, as well as corporate overhead. For variable costs per unit, companies seek to improve their materials purchasing/mix, labor efficiency, manufacturing processes, and technology. For fixed overhead, companies strive to control corporate expenses such as salaries, administrative, and rent.

Auto suppliers make more money as the OEMs produce more vehicles, including backlog build. Beyond volumes, Delphi's sales growth was driven by increased content per vehicle and product mix. Therefore, we scrutinized key trends in technology, environmental and safety standards, and innovations.

For pricing, auto suppliers are generally subject to price-downs, which are contracted annual selling price reductions to the OEMs. Some of Delphi's peers were subject to price-downs of 3% to 4%. For Delphi, we assumed a more modest 2% drag on annual sales growth supported by its recent track record and "critical-needs" products.

Monthly auto sales volumes are widely reported in terms of SAAR (seasonally adjusted annual rate). Given Delphi's diversified geographic exposure, regional SAAR analysis was needed for Europe, North America, Asia Pacific, and South America. As shown in Exhibit 3.2, the global auto sales recovery was in full swing by 2011. Emerging market volumes, particularly in China (captured in Asia Pacific), were expected to grow by nearly 50% over the next five years. This was highly beneficial for Delphi given its strong Chinese presence.

EXHIBIT 3.2 Global Light Vehicle Volumes
(units in millions)

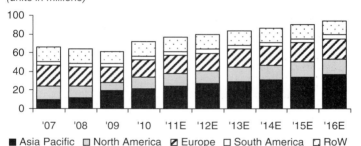

■ Asia Pacific □ North America ▨ Europe □ South America □ RoW

Source: IHS Automotive and Barclays Capital

Delphi's growing backlog and design wins on new platforms further supported these trends. The company was strategically investing in next-generation technologies to drive long-term growth, as demonstrated by its healthy projected capex spend (see Exhibit 3.11). OEM trends towards supplier base consolidation and global car platforms also positioned preferred partners like Delphi for market share gains.

On the content side, tightening fuel economy (see Exhibit 3.3) and safety standards were driving higher content per vehicle. This was further augmented by demand for increased connectivity, electronics, infotainment, and active safety systems exemplified by the increasing trends towards telematics (see Exhibit 3.4).

EXHIBIT 3.3 Fuel Economy Standards by Geography
(miles per gallon)

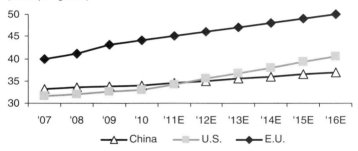

Source: International Council on Clean Transportation (ICCT)

EXHIBIT 3.4 Installation Rates of Embedded Telematics
(% of production volume)

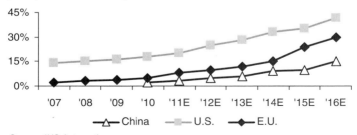

Source: IHS Automotive

On the profitability side, Delphi's margin opportunity appeared just as compelling as its growth story. The company was becoming increasingly disciplined in its bidding for new business, which created a higher-quality backlog and product mix for Delphi. Our analysis suggested that the company was positioned to realize several hundred basis points (bps)[2] of margin improvement in the coming years due to:

- *Product mix shift* – focus on higher-margin products tied to electrification, connectivity, and safety

- *BCCs* – ongoing migration of manufacturing base to best-cost regions, over 90% at time of IPO

- *Flexible workforce* – ability to "flex" to market conditions, 70% variable cost structure and no UAW (United Automobile Workers union)

- *Lean savings* – deep-seated continuous improvement culture driven by management and the Board, resulting in one of the "leanest" cost structures in the sector

- *Pricing* – emphasis on premium pricing, which was supported by disciplined bidding, product quality, and stickiness

- *Operating leverage* – ability to leverage fixed cost base across increasing volumes

- *Emerging markets* – penetration of high-margin products combined with leverage over OEMs

---

[2] A basis point represents 1/100th of a percentage point.

III. What is its moat & competitive position?

Quality businesses tend to have sustainable competitive advantages over their peers and high barriers to entry. This is commonly referred to as a "moat." Differentiated products, intellectual property, scale, brand, sticky customer relationships, low-cost structure, and high upfront capital investment all support the resilience of a business model.

Industries with fewer competitors and high barriers to entry have greater prospects for outperformance. Companies that face fierce competition risk lower growth, profitability, and diminishing returns. This is especially true when participants engage in irrational behavior to gain market share. Also, be mindful that industries currently generating high returns on capital may attract new entrants. So, even top-performing companies can never get complacent.

Fortunately for Delphi, its moat was well-defined. Key barriers included:

- *Low-cost structure* – arguably the leanest cost structure in the industry with an average hourly wage of $7, resulting from its BCC-heavy footprint, local sourcing, and no UAW exposure

- *Market leadership & global scale* – holds top or secondary market position for most of its core products; operates 110 manufacturing facilities in 30 countries; 16,000+ scientists, engineers, and technicians focused on R&D

- *Spec'd-in products* – direct collaboration with OEMs to develop innovative and tailored solutions with differentiated technology; Delphi products are designed into new vehicle platforms years before launch date, resulting in sizable backlog and high switching costs; products found in vast majority of top-selling models globally

- *Customer relationships* – decades-long collaboration with major OEMs; 15 strategically located technical centers dedicated to product development, complemented by on-site design and engineering teams at customer locations

- *China* – market leader in China with long-standing presence dating back to 1992 serving both domestic and foreign OEMs; expects roughly 50% of future growth to be generated from emerging markets

From a competitive perspective, Delphi contended with multiple global players in each segment, as disclosed in the S-1 (see Exhibit 3.5).

EXHIBIT 3.5 Competitors by Segment

Segment	Competitors
Electrical/Electronic Architecture	Leoni, Molex, TE Connectivity, Sumitomo, Yazaki
Powertrain Systems	BorgWarner, Bosch, Continental, Denso, Hitachi, Magneti Marelli
Electronics & Safety	Aisin, Autoliv, Bosch, Continental, Denso, Harman, Panasonic
Thermal Systems	Denso, MAHLE Behr, Sanden, Valeo, Visteon

Delphi's competitive advantages varied by segment. For Electrical/Electronic Architecture, the company was an innovator in optimizing product weight and cost. In Powertrain, its technological know-how and R&D enabled it to go toe-to-toe with the likes of German-engineering heavyweights Bosch and Conti. And, in Electronics & Safety, Delphi was a leader in active safety, infotainment, and user experience systems.

IV. How strong are customer & supplier relationships?

To understand a business, you must study its position in the value chain. In other words, how powerful is its standing vis-à-vis customers and suppliers? This analysis centers on concentration, tenure, negotiating power, and other relationship dynamics.

Customers

A company's fortunes are directly tied to those of its customers. When concentration is high, customer disruption or a major contract loss can be disastrous. Furthermore, a company's ability to negotiate favorable terms may be limited vs. one whose customer base is fragmented. A public company often discloses its top customers and concentration under a "Business" or "Customers" section in the 10-K.

High concentration requires in-depth customer diligence. This work is similar to that for the actual investment opportunity. Follow key customers' performance trends, outlook, and financial health.

Customer due diligence also involves the length of the relationships. In general, the longer the better as evidence of stickiness and durability. While a single customer representing 20% of sales may raise eyebrows, you get more comfortable if the relationship has been in place for decades.

You also want to look at specific relationship dynamics. For example, if product switching costs are high or the customer has few alternatives, you gain confidence in the stickiness factor.

Per Delphi's S-1, its top 10 customers comprised over 65% of total sales with the top 3 customers representing 38% (see Exhibit 3.6).

EXHIBIT 3.6 Delphi Customer List

Customer	% of Sales
General Motors (GM)	21%
Ford Motor Company	9%
Volkswagen Group	8%
Daimler AG	6%
PSA Peugeot Citroën	5%
Renault SA	4%
Shanghai GM	4%
Fiat Group	3%
Hyundai Kia Automotive	3%
Toyota Motor Corporation	3%

While not too alarming, this level of concentration required scrutiny. Fortunately, Delphi's relationships with its top customers went back decades. The track record was time-tested. For the most part, its key customers also had strong credit profiles, with most rated investment grade.

Perhaps most reassuring, Delphi pledged increased customer diversification to IPO investors in late 2011. Management stated that no customer would account for more than 15% of sales going forward. Delphi's buyback of GM's $4.3 billion equity stake earlier in the year gave further comfort to IPO investors that their largest customer's influence would lessen over time.

Delphi also laid out a geographic diversification plan whereby it would target a 30% / 30% / 30% / 10% regional balance for North America / Europe / Asia-Pacific / South America. This compared to a 33% / 43% / 16% / 8% mix at the IPO.

Suppliers

As with heavy reliance on a few customers, you need to be mindful of supplier concentration. Large suppliers tend to have substantial leverage over their customers, which heightens the risk of aggressive behavior. This is especially true for hard-to-get materials or sole-source situations. In general, investors need to be mindful when the supplier-provided inputs or services comprise a significant portion of the company's cost of goods sold (COGS).[3]

---

[3]COGS are the direct expenses associated with producing the products and services provided by the company. Typical COGS include materials, labor, distribution, and manufacturing costs.

Some companies specifically list their key suppliers in the 10-K or prospectus, while others note their exposure to certain raw materials. Common raw materials include metals (e.g., aluminum, copper, steel) and petroleum products (e.g., oil, gas, resins). A company that relies on one or two suppliers is susceptible to their material shortages and operational disruptions.

While Delphi doesn't explicitly list its supplier and raw material exposure in its S-1, it does note that:

> *"We procure our raw materials from a variety of suppliers around the world. Generally, we seek to obtain materials in the region in which our products are manufactured in order to minimize transportation and other costs. The most significant raw materials we use to manufacture our products include aluminum, copper and resins."*

Like Delphi's customer concentration, this heavy commodity exposure merited scrutiny. Fortunately, its list of global suppliers was deep and diverse. The company's global footprint also enabled it to source locally, as appropriate. We saw the larger risk as related to underlying commodity price volatility and Delphi's ability to pass through spikes. As we discuss later, however, Delphi was effective at mitigating this exposure through pass-through contracts and hedging.

V. What are the primary risks to the business?

Operational Risks

You must constantly be on the look-out for risks to your thesis. We have already touched on many of the operational risks facing companies, namely cyclical exposure, competitive pressures, customer/supplier issues, and escalating input costs. To those, we need to add currency movements, technological obsolescence, and financial leverage.

As noted in Delphi's S-1, its *operational risks* include:

- **Production Volume** – "*Automotive sales and production are highly cyclical. Lower global auto sales result in our OEM customers lowering production, which has a direct impact on our cash flows. The most recent example of this was the 2009 downturn in which North American and Western Europe auto production declined 43% and 26%, respectively, below levels in 2007.*"

- **Competition** – "*We operate in the highly competitive automotive supply industry. Competition is based primarily on price, technology, quality, delivery and overall customer service.*" Competition is a reality in every industry. Even for those industries with a benign competitive environment today, tomorrow may bring new unforeseen entrants.

- **Customers** – "*Declines in the market share or business of our five largest customers may have a disproportionate adverse impact on our revenues and profitability.*" Concentration exposes a company to problems at key customers, including operational issues or financial struggles.

- **Suppliers** – "*Any significant disruption in our supplier relationships, particularly relationships with sole-source suppliers, could harm our profitability.*" As with customers, supplier concentration represents heightened vulnerability to third parties.

- **Input Costs** – "*In recent periods there have been significant fluctuations in the global prices of copper, aluminum and petroleum-based resin products, and fuel charges, which have had an unfavorable impact on our business.*" Adverse swings in key raw material prices can meaningfully impact financial results. Delphi used a combination of hedging and contractual pass-through agreements with customers to help mitigate this risk.

- **Currency** – "*Currency exposures may impact future cash flows. ~65% of our 2010 revenue was invoiced in currencies other than the U.S. dollar ... [most notably] the Mexican Peso, Euro, Chinese Yuan, Turkish Lira and Great British Pound.*" While Delphi's reported USD sales and earnings were impacted by FX, its margins were typically protected given its strategy of matching sales and costs in the same currency.

- **Emerging Technologies** – "*We may not be able to respond quickly enough to changes in regulations and technological risks, and to develop our intellectual property into commercially viable products.*" All businesses must live with the threat of substitute technologies that alter the value proposition of existing products and services.

- **Leverage/Liquidity** – "*A prolonged economic downturn or economic uncertainty could adversely affect our business and cause us to require additional sources of financing, which may not be available.*" Companies need to manage their balance sheets and liquidity to create sufficient cushion for downturns. This typically comes in the form of revolver capacity, cash on hand, and a prudent debt load and *maturity schedule.*[4]

---

[4] Companies should seek to have a balanced debt maturity schedule that is spaced out over several years vs. all coming due at the same time (see later in this chapter, *Financial Due Diligence: III. Is the balance sheet healthy?*).

Once you identify the key risks, you seek to quantify them to inform your investment decision. In Exhibit 3.7, we show Delphi's sensitivities to moves in production volumes and EUR/USD exchange rates, as well as copper and oil prices. For each percentage move in the underlying risk factor, we show the corresponding impact on sales and EBITDA.

EXHIBIT 3.7 Risk Sensitivity Analysis

		Impact	
Item	**Sensitivity**	**Sales**	**EBITDA**
Volume	+/- 1%	+/- $150m	+/- $40m
EUR	+/- 10%	+/- $650m	+/- $65m
Copper Price	+/- 10%	+/- $85m	+/- $15m
Oil Price	+/- 10%	−	+/- $25m

Non-operational Risks

You must also identify non-business-related risks to your thesis. These may be regulatory, geopolitical, environmental, or legal. Often, these risks are more difficult to foresee than the operational ones. That does not, however, let you off the hook.

Non-operational risks are particularly relevant for companies in certain industries and geographies. For Delphi, the auto supply industry has a well-documented history of product recall and environmental regulatory issues. In addition, its sizable operations in China carry emerging markets and country-specific geopolitical risk.

As disclosed in Delphi's S-1, its *non-operational risks* include:

- **Regulatory** – "*We may not be able to respond quickly enough to changes in regulations.*" Unanticipated changes in regulations, rules, or laws always loom as a potential threat.

- **Geopolitical** – "*We face risks associated with doing business in non-U.S. jurisdictions…Our business in China is…sensitive to economic and market conditions.*" Substantive operations in "high-risk" countries represent a key concern as they increase susceptibility to domestic unrest, regime changes, business climate uncertainties, sanctions, and even tariffs.

- **Environmental** – "*We may be adversely affected by…environmental regulation, litigation or other liabilities.*" Environmental risks are typically specific to the industry. For example, asbestos-related lawsuits resulted in multi-billion dollar penalties and some notable bankruptcies in the industrials sector from the 1980s through the early 2000s.

- **Legal** – "*We may incur material losses and costs as a result of warranty claims, product recalls, product liability and intellectual property infringement actions.*" Investors must live with the reality of legal risk for all their holdings. In autos, product failures and recalls are particularly relevant.

Existential Risks

Existential threats endanger a company's very existence. Emerging disruptive technologies constantly threaten age-old business models. As part of your diligence, you need to gain comfort that the company is well-positioned to withstand technological change. This same analysis can also be used to identify short ideas.

Ideally the company is at the forefront of innovation and itself a disruptor. This is how the New Delphi positioned itself. The company's vision and courage to embrace automobile electrification and connectivity early on set up Delphi for success in the coming decade.

In the retail sector, the demise of both Blockbuster Video and Borders Group are high-profile examples of companies that were upended by disruptive technologies. Blockbuster, the video rental retailer, generated sales of $6 billion and EBITDA of $500 million in 2004. By 2010, however, its sales and EBITDA had declined to $3.25 billion and -$20 million, respectively. What happened? Did people lose interest in watching movies at home? Of course not. A new method for delivering movies to viewers' living rooms emerged, but Blockbuster failed to evolve.

The primary disruptor was Netflix, which first offered DVD-by-mail rentals and then adapted to offer online video streaming. Over the same 2004 to 2010 timeframe, Netflix's sales of $500 million and EBITDA of $25 million increased to $2.2 billion and $325 million, respectively. Blockbuster ultimately filed for bankruptcy in September 2010 while NFLX saw its share price rise from a split-adjusted $1 at its 2002 IPO to $25 by the end of 2010. By year-end 2019, its share price was $324.

Borders, the book and music retailer, experienced a similar fate at the hands of e-commerce juggernaut Amazon.com. In 2005, Borders generated sales of nearly $4 billion and EBITDA of $300 million, which fell to $2.2 billion and -$200 million, respectively, by 2010.

Why? Did people lose interest in reading books? On the contrary, book sales soared but Amazon reaped the rewards. Borders failed to adapt its business model and ultimately filed for bankruptcy in January 2012. Meanwhile, AMZN saw its share price rise from a split-adjusted $2 at its 1997 IPO to over $250 by the end of 2012. By year-end 2019, its share price was $1,848.

Financial Due Diligence

Financial due diligence centers on the analysis and interpretation of a company's historical and projected financial performance. It goes hand in hand with business due diligence. Both are necessary and neither alone is sufficient.

While some math skills are required, the good news is that the basics suffice—addition, subtraction, multiplication, and division. It also helps to be able to navigate your way through the three primary financial statements—income statement, balance sheet, and cash flow statement. The ability to use Microsoft Excel is highly beneficial, if not a prerequisite.

Given the basic math, the easy part is performing the actual calculations. The hard part comes afterwards in the interpretation of the data. What is driving the company's performance? Why is the company out/underperforming its peers? Is it sustainable? How will competitors react? What will performance look like over the next one, two, five, or even ten years. Ultimately, your analysis seeks to provide comfort on future performance, which of course is never certain.

As with business diligence, we provide a five-question checklist for performing financial due diligence (see Exhibit 3.8).

EXHIBIT 3.8 Financial Due Diligence Checklist

Financial Due Diligence Checklist

I. Where has the company been?

II. Where is it going?

III. Is the balance sheet healthy?

IV. Does it generate strong free cash flow?

V. How does management allocate capital?

I. Where has the company been?

First, you need to focus on the company's historical performance. How and why did it experience growing, flat, or declining sales and profitability? Typically, a three-to-five-year historical period is sufficient to form conclusions, especially if it spans prior cycles. Make sure the numbers are "clean," i.e., properly adjusted for one-time items and any M&A. You also need to compare these trends against peers and understand the differences.

We noted earlier that your diligence needs to have the flexibility to uncover turnarounds and fixer-uppers. Having recently emerged from bankruptcy, Delphi clearly fell into this bucket. Its Chapter 11 filing in 2005 was the product of an uncompetitive cost structure, excess debt, and burdensome pension liabilities. At the time, Delphi had negative EBITDA and liabilities totaling approximately $22 billion. The company was bleeding cash with no clear path to covering its ongoing interest, pension, and operating expenses.

As a side note, only Delphi's U.S. assets were subject to the Chapter 11 filing. While the U.S. turnaround story grabbed most of the headlines, the European restructuring project was no less impressive. Delphi transformed its European business into an earnings machine with double-digit margins that were previously unheard of. This was driven by a best-cost manufacturing base in Northern Africa and Eastern Europe, an hourly workforce comprised of 30% temps, and the successful sourcing of engineering talent from BCCs, such as Poland.

During its multi-year bankruptcy, Delphi dramatically reduced its product lines from 119 down to 33. No less important, the company chose to focus on areas where it was best positioned to win, exiting 11 businesses, including the Steering and Passive Safety segments. By summer 2009, Delphi's lead shareholders negotiated an agreement with GM to take back its remaining U.S. unionized plants.

The resulting New Delphi featured a clean balance sheet, right-sized cost structure, and streamlined product portfolio. From a purely financial point of view, bankruptcy also enabled Delphi to lower its corporate tax rate to 20%. Lower taxes meant higher conversion of operating income to EPS and FCF. This provided a clear advantage vs. U.S. peers who were subject to higher rates.

As shown in Exhibit 3.9, after a dramatic downturn from 2007 through 2009, the company's fortunes started to improve. In 2010, sales increased 17.5% and were on pace for similar growth in 2011. What drove this massive sales increase? Fortunately, helpful color was provided in the MD&A[5] of Delphi's 2011 S-1:

---

[5]Management's Discussion and Analysis. Mandatory SEC filing disclosure that provides an overview of the prior reporting period's financial performance, and typically trends and outlook.

"Our improved sales reflect the impacts of increased OEM production as well as the level of our content per unit. These improvements continue to indicate a stabilization of the global economy. However, volumes in North America and Western Europe continue to be substantially less than [those] prior to 2008 and 2009."

Now let's look at Delphi's profitability, which followed a parallel path. Gross margins improved dramatically from a 2009 low of 1.9% to 15.7% in 2011E. Net income went from -$866 million to +$1.1 billion. And, the company started generating substantial FCF. Per the MD&A:

"In 2010, we largely completed our restructuring activities, resulting in a lower fixed cost base, improved manufacturing footprint and reduced overhead. We dramatically reduced our U.S. and Western European footprints, realigned our SG&A cost structure and increased the variable nature of our employee base."

Delphi's newly flexible labor force and operating leverage were critical profit drivers. Further, the company was benefiting from an improved commodity price environment. But was this success sustainable?

EXHIBIT 3.9 Delphi Five-Year Historical Financial Summary – Income Statement and Free Cash Flow

($ in millions, except per share data)

Delphi Five-Year Historical Financial Summary – Income Statement and Free Cash Flow

	Historical Period				2011E	CAGR ('07 – '11)
	2007	2008	2009	2010		
Sales by Segment						
Electrical Architecture	$5,968	$5,649	$4,295	$5,620	$6,622	2.6%
Powertrain Systems	$5,663	$5,368	$3,624	$4,086	$4,918	(3.5%)
Electronics & Safety	$5,035	$4,048	$2,562	$2,721	$2,955	(12.5%)
Thermal Systems	$2,412	$2,121	$1,373	$1,603	$1,796	(7.1%)
Income Statement						
Sales	$19,526	$16,808	$11,755	$13,817	$16,039	(4.8%)
% growth	1.0%	(13.9%)	(30.1%)	17.5%	16.1%	
Gross Profit	$883	$651	$228	$2,049	$2,526	30.0%
% margin	4.5%	3.9%	1.9%	14.8%	15.7%	
EBITDA	$731	$269	$84	$1,633	$2,044	29.3%
% margin	3.7%	1.6%	0.7%	11.8%	12.7%	
% growth	NM	NM	NM	NM	25.2%	
D&A	$871	$822	$679	$421	$478	
Interest Expense	764	434	8	30	123	(13.9%)
Net Income	($1,760)	($2,013)	($866)	$631	$1,072	(36.7%)
Diluted Shares (1)	686	686	686	686	328	
EPS	($2.57)	($2.93)	($1.26)	$0.92	$3.27	NM
% growth	NM	NM	NM	NM	255.0%	
Cash Flow Statement						
Cash from Operations	($98)	$455	($98)	$1,142	$1,356	NM
Less: Capex	(577)	(771)	(409)	(500)	(629)	
% of sales	3.0%	4.6%	3.5%	3.6%	3.9%	
Free Cash Flow	($675)	($316)	($507)	$642	$727	NM
FCF / S	($0.98)	($0.46)	($0.74)	$0.94	$2.21	NM
% growth	NM	NM	NM	NM	136.7%	NM

(1) 2011E diluted shares as of IPO date.

II. Where is it going?

Now that you know where the company has been, it's time to figure out where it is going. Try to visualize what the company will look like over the next one, two, five, or even ten years. Growth expectations are critical for valuation. Equity investors tend to reward faster-growing companies with higher trading multiples than slower-growing peers. They also focus on organic vs. acquisition-driven growth, with the former generally viewed more favorably.

Growth refers to sales and earnings. Investors look for both. Sales growth without earnings growth raises obvious cost questions. Similarly, earnings growth without sales growth raises questions about sustainability. There's only so much cost to squeeze out of the lemon.

The company's growth outlook needs to be reflected in the financial model, typically five years of projections. The goal is to project the highest probability outcome. Inevitably there will be deviations. But, if the core assumptions are well-researched and vetted, the chances for dispersion narrow.

While the future is inherently uncertain, you need to look for clues. Start with the most recent earnings call transcripts, MD&A, and investor presentations. Many companies also provide guidance in the form of a range. Your view on management capability and credibility will inform your interpretation. Sell-side research and consensus estimates offer further perspective, particularly from the most well-regarded analysts.

Regardless of where guidance or consensus falls, you need to do your own work. In some cases, "consensus" masks a wide disparity between the individual analyst estimates that comprise it. Therefore, it is essential to develop an understanding of the company's key financial drivers and model accordingly.

To craft financial projections, start by revisiting the work you did in the prior section. Focus on historical growth rates for sales, EBITDA, and EPS, as well as margin trends. Only then can you start to look forward. Will growth continue at the same trajectory, accelerate, or decelerate?

As previously discussed, often two or three key variables drive financial performance and hence the projections. Recall that Delphi's sales are largely a function of global production volumes by region, backlog, and price. Therefore, annual sales projections are typically based on forward-looking third-party production data, new business/backlog growth, and price-downs.

For profitability projections, investors focus on gross profit, EBITDA, and net income. Gross profit, defined as sales less COGS, is the profit earned after subtracting costs directly related to the production of products and services. COGS are largely *variable* and correlated to the volume of goods or services sold. Gross margin is calculated as gross profit as a percentage of sales.

A detailed modeling approach for gross profit projects COGS based on price and volume for key expense inputs. Delphi's key COGS primarily include materials and labor with additional costs relating to manufacturing overhead and freight. A "quick and dirty" approach, on the other hand, assumes gross margin as a % of sales based on recent trends, independent research, or management guidance.

The same holds true for modeling EBITDA and EBIT, which are net of COGS and SG&A (selling, general & administrative expenses), a.k.a., corporate overhead. The detailed approach projects SG&A as a separate line item and subtracts it from gross profit to calculate EBIT.[6] You then add back D&A expense to solve for EBITDA. D&A is often projected as a percentage of sales based on historical levels.

SG&A expense is largely *fixed* and often modeled by growing it at GDP or an "inflation-plus" rate. Or, SG&A can be modeled as a percentage of sales in line with recent trends. For either approach, be mindful of major cost-cutting or expansion initiatives, which can significantly impact this line item.

---

[6] The EBIT calculation assumes that D&A expense is included in COGS and, to a lesser extent, SG&A.

For net income, you need to factor in interest expense and taxes. To the extent these expenses are dynamic, it is prudent to model them separately rather than relying on high level margin assumptions. This is particularly important for levered companies that are repaying debt and hence lowering their interest expense going forward. It is also applicable for companies that are raising debt to repurchase shares or fund growth.

For per share metrics, most notably EPS and FCF/S, you divide the numerators—net income and free cash flow, respectively—by diluted shares. For the denominator, keep in mind potential stock buybacks, issuances, or other corporate actions that could impact the future share count.

Exhibit 3.10 displays our specific model assumptions for Delphi. They reference historical performance as well as production outlook by geography, backlog estimates, and standard pricing reductions. Per Exhibit 3.11, these assumptions resulted in sales growing at a 6%+ CAGR over the next five years. Gross margins surpassed 17.5% by the end of the projection period, while EBITDA margins reached 14.5%.

Further, we modeled EPS and FCF/S growing meaningfully faster than revenue and EBITDA due to a reduced share count from stock buybacks. Our buyback assumptions started at $250 million in Year 1 and scaled to $750 million by Year 5.

EXHIBIT 3.10 Summary Model Assumptions

($ in millions)

Summary Model Assumptions					
		Projection Period			
	2012E	2013E	2014E	2015E	2016E
Sales Drivers					
Light Vehicle Production (000s)					
North America	13,907	14,880	15,624	16,093	16,576
Europe	18,527	19,268	19,846	20,442	21,055
South America	4,394	4,526	4,617	4,663	4,686
China	18,544	19,842	22,216	23,786	25,071
Geographic Exposure					
North America	34%	34%	34%	34%	33%
Europe	39%	38%	37%	37%	37%
South America	8%	8%	8%	7%	7%
China	20%	20%	21%	22%	22%
Incremental Backlog	$900	$900	$1,000	$1,000	$1,000
Price-downs	(2%)	(2%)	(2%)	(2%)	(2%)
Costs & Expenditures					
COGS as % of sales	83.9%	83.4%	82.9%	82.7%	82.4%
SG&A % of sales	5.5%	5.5%	5.5%	5.5%	5.5%
D&A % of sales	3.0%	3.0%	3.0%	3.0%	3.0%
Capex % of sales	4.5%	4.5%	4.5%	4.5%	4.5%
Capital Allocation					
Buybacks	$250	$350	$450	$500	$750
Dividends	–	–	–	–	–

EXHIBIT 3.11 Delphi Five-Year Projected Financial Summary – Income Statement and Free Cash Flow

($ in millions, except per share data)

Delphi Five-Year Projected Financial Summary – Income Statement and Free Cash Flow						
			Projection Period			CAGR
	2012E	2013E	2014E	2015E	2016E	('11 - '16)
Sales by Segment						
Electrical Architecture	$6,817	$7,319	$7,852	$8,269	$8,662	5.5%
Powertrain Systems	$5,145	$5,633	$6,108	$6,478	$6,885	7.0%
Electronics & Safety	$3,053	$3,374	$3,703	$3,987	$4,267	7.6%
Thermal Systems	$1,854	$1,983	$2,139	$2,263	$2,379	5.8%
Income Statement						
Sales	$16,594	$18,023	$19,507	$20,691	$21,879	6.4%
% growth	*3.5%*	*8.6%*	*8.2%*	*6.1%*	*5.7%*	
Gross Profit	$2,671	$2,991	$3,335	$3,589	$3,850	8.8%
% margin	*16.1%*	*16.6%*	*17.1%*	*17.3%*	*17.6%*	
EBITDA	$2,157	$2,433	$2,731	$2,948	$3,172	9.2%
% margin	*13.0%*	*13.5%*	*14.0%*	*14.2%*	*14.5%*	
% growth	*5.5%*	*12.8%*	*12.2%*	*8.0%*	*7.6%*	
D&A	$490	$532	$575	$610	$645	7.2%
Interest Expense	123	121	120	119	117	(1.3%)
Net Income	$1,180	$1,371	$1,577	$1,726	$1,882	11.9%
Diluted Shares	324	314	304	294	284	
EPS	$3.65	$4.36	$5.19	$5.87	$6.64	15.2%
% growth	*11.7%*	*19.7%*	*19.0%*	*13.2%*	*12.9%*	
Cash Flow Statement						
Cash from Operations	$1,639	$1,836	$2,083	$2,282	$2,472	12.8%
Less: Capex	(747)	(811)	(878)	(931)	(985)	
% of sales	*4.5%*	*4.5%*	*4.5%*	*4.5%*	*4.5%*	
Free Cash Flow	$892	$1,025	$1,205	$1,351	$1,487	15.4%
FCF / S	$2.76	$3.26	$3.97	$4.60	$5.24	18.8%
% growth	*24.5%*	*18.4%*	*21.5%*	*15.9%*	*14.1%*	

III. Is the balance sheet healthy?

A strong balance sheet is essential for a healthy business. It provides flexibility for growing operations, both organically and through M&A, as well as for capital returns. It also provides a buffer during difficult times. Conversely, a weak balance sheet constrains growth, limits access to external capital, and reduces the margin for error.

To understand a company's balance sheet, you need to explore its capital structure and key credit statistics. Capital structure refers to the amount, components, and terms of a company's debt and equity. The more debt, the greater the risk. As witnessed during the run-up to the Great Recession, many sophisticated investors underestimated the perils of a stretched balance sheet.

Capital structure affects both financial and operational performance. Higher leverage means higher interest expense, which negatively impacts earnings and cash flow. A challenged capital structure may also mean less funds for operations. On a more extreme level, it leads to liquidity problems and potentially bankruptcy.

In the event of bankruptcy, equity investors suffer severe impairment or total loss as they occupy the most junior position in the capital structure. Unlike lenders, shareholders have neither guaranteed interest payments nor contractual principal repayment at a set maturity date. As noted in Step II, equity investors tend to prefer lower leverage and higher coverage.

Equity investors also need to be cognizant of when a company's debt comes due, i.e., the debt maturity schedule. Upon maturity, debt obligations must be refinanced with fresh capital from the market or retired with cash on hand. If not, then the company will be in default. The inability to refinance or repay debt may be due to poor financial performance or weak capital markets, or both. Regardless, the result is often bankruptcy.

From a balance sheet perspective, Delphi emerged from bankruptcy with a significantly improved credit profile. At the time of the IPO, leverage was reduced to 1x and the company's $1.45 billion cash balance meant that leverage was only 0.3x on a net basis. A new $1.3 billion undrawn revolver also bolstered the company's liquidity profile. Further, the company had no significant debt maturities over the next five years.

This positioned Delphi for strong organic and inorganic growth. Its balance sheet capacity could be used for R&D/capital projects, M&A, buybacks, and dividends. Going forward, we modeled Delphi's credit profile continuing to improve through EBITDA growth and mandatory debt repayment (see Exhibit 3.12).

EXHIBIT 3.12 Delphi Five-Year Projected Financial Summary – Balance Sheet Summary

($ in millions)

Delphi Five-Year Projected Financial Summary – Balance Sheet Summary			Projection Period			
	2011E	2012E	2013E	2014E	2015E	2016E
Financial Statistics						
EBITDA	$2,044	$2,157	$2,433	$2,731	$2,948	$3,172
Interest Expense	123	123	121	120	119	117
Capital Expenditures	629	747	811	878	931	985
% of sales	3.9%	4.5%	4.5%	4.5%	4.5%	4.5%
Capital Structure						
Cash	$1,455	$2,012	$2,651	$3,370	$4,185	$4,802
Secured Debt	1,042	956	920	884	848	728
Total Debt	2,114	2,028	1,992	1,956	1,920	1,800
Net Debt	658	16	(659)	(1,414)	(2,265)	(3,002)
Credit Statistics						
Coverage						
EBITDA / Int. Exp.	16.6x	17.5x	20.0x	22.7x	24.8x	27.2x
(EBITDA - Capex) / Int.	11.5x	11.5x	13.4x	15.4x	16.9x	18.7x
Leverage						
Secured Debt / EBITDA	0.5x	0.4x	0.4x	0.3x	0.3x	0.2x
Total Debt / EBITDA	1.0x	0.9x	0.8x	0.7x	0.7x	0.6x
Net Debt / EBITDA	0.3x	0.0x	(0.3x)	(0.5x)	(0.8x)	(0.9x)
Working Capital						
Net Working Capital	$587	$613	$675	$739	$789	$839
% of sales	3.7%	3.7%	3.7%	3.8%	3.8%	3.8%

Leverage, of course, is not all bad. Used properly, it can be a powerful value driver. Debt is inherently cheaper than equity and is often the optimal way to fund growth ... up to a point. Therefore, be sure to analyze balance sheet capacity when evaluating an opportunity.

Additional debt can be used to repurchase shares or fund M&A, thereby increasing EPS. For a company with 1.5x leverage vs. peers at 2.5x, you can model in 1x incremental leverage to fund a buyback or make an acquisition. Then, assess pro forma EPS for each scenario. This analysis helps identify potential catalysts. For Delphi, at only 1x total leverage post-IPO, we saw potential for buybacks beyond what we modeled, as well as future M&A.

IV. Does it generate strong free cash flow?

Free cash flow is the lifeblood of a company. It is the cash generated after paying all cash expenses—COGS, SG&A, interest, and associated taxes—as well as the funding of capex and working capital. As such, it denotes a company's ability to invest in growth, return capital to shareholders, or repay debt. For many investors, P/FCF or FCF yield is the primary valuation basis on which they invest.

Investors analyze the percentage of EBITDA or net income that gets converted into cash flow. You may see a company report that FCF exceeded net income, a powerful signal. Ideally, this is due to low capex requirements or working capital efficiency. However, be on the look-out for FCF that is inflated due to one-time items, underinvestment, or temporary tax benefits. Similarly, a company with strong earnings but consistently weak FCF may portend trouble ahead.

FCF generation is driven by multiple factors, with profitability being foremost among them. Margins for gross profit, EBITDA, and EBIT show a company's operating profitability. Net income goes one step further, netting out financial charges such as interest expense and taxes. However, even a high margin business can have a poor FCF profile if its capital intensity is too high. Capital intensity refers to cash spending needs for maintenance and growth initiatives, most notably capex and working capital.

Capex are the funds that a company uses to purchase, improve, expand, or replace PP&E. Historical levels help guide projections for future capex. Note that these projections may deviate from historical levels depending on the company's strategy or phase of operations. A company in expansion mode might have elevated capex for some portion of the projection period. Fortunately, planned capex is typically discussed in the 10-K or on earnings calls.

It is also important to differentiate between expenditures deemed necessary to continue operating the business ("maintenance capex") and those that are discretionary ("growth capex"). Companies typically get the benefit of the doubt that growth capex can be curtailed in difficult times. For Delphi, we modeled capex increasing from just under 4% in 2011 to 4.5% of sales throughout the projection period given planned investments in new product launches (see Exhibit 3.12).

Net working capital (NWC) is the cash needed to fund a company's operations on an ongoing basis. It is the sum of the cash tied up in credit sales and inventory ("current assets") *minus* the cash owed to vendors ("current liabilities"). As a general rule, heavy NWC requirements are looked upon unfavorably. Capital tied up in accounts receivable and inventory means less cash available to the company and its shareholders.

Investors look at a variety of metrics to measure NWC efficiency. Perhaps the simplest is NWC as a percentage of sales. Year-over-year trends are particularly telling. A notable increase in NWC as a % of sales may be a warning sign. Meaningful NWC efficiency improvements, on the other hand, bolster a company's FCF profile. For Delphi, we assumed NWC at a relatively flat 3.7% to 3.8% of sales throughout the projection period.

Given the above, in conjunction with its accelerating volumes and increased profitability, Delphi's FCF generation outlook was strong. Per Exhibit 3.11, we modeled Delphi's FCF to accelerate meaningfully during the projection period.

V. How does management allocate capital?

Effective capital allocation is a key differentiator for best-in-class companies. Disciplined management teams continuously assess the relative returns on their allocation of capital. In other words, what is the highest return for each dollar spent? The most prevalent ways to deploy cash include:

- Organic growth projects

- Mergers & acquisitions

- Share repurchases

- Dividends

- Debt repayment

Skeptical that capital allocation is a core value driver? Well, consider the following. For both Blockbuster and Borders, imagine a world where they decided early on to allocate capital to digital or online solutions vs. increasing their storefronts. Perhaps they would still be alive today.

Companies typically look first to allocate capital to internal opportunities. Organic growth projects are viewed as lower risk. These initiatives may come in the form of new facilities, locations, machinery, R&D, product introductions, or technology platforms.

Companies may also look externally at M&A opportunities as the best use of cash. Strategic fit and price paid are obviously critical here, as is the acquirer's track record. Does the company have a strong history of executing accretive deals and delivering on announced synergies? Are the potential targets strategic and value-enhancing?

Other capital allocation strategies focus on direct return of capital, most notably stock buybacks and dividends. Here, track record is also important. For prior buybacks, analyze how much stock the company repurchased and at what prices. For companies announcing first-time buybacks, your analysis should center on balance sheet capacity and pro forma EPS.

A company's dividend strategy requires similar analytics. Does the company pay regular dividends or large one-time payments as cash accumulates? For how long has the company paid a dividend and has it been increasing? What is the current dividend yield? Is the dividend a meaningful portion of net income, as reflected in its payout ratio? A company with a 50% payout ratio and consistent 3% to 4% yield is more likely to get investors' attention.

Debt repayment can also enhance shareholder returns. This is especially true for a quality company with a heavy debt load but a clear path to deleveraging. Sponsor-backed IPOs (former LBOs that have gone public) and highly cyclical companies merit attention in this respect. Accelerated debt repayment via FCF results in lower interest expense and hence higher EPS. Furthermore, deleveraging may re-rate the company with a higher multiple as it de-risks the equity and creates capacity for growth.

For Delphi, we modeled FCF funding buybacks in the absence of M&A. This was a notable upgrade from the Old Delphi, which had a long-standing reputation among equity investors as an unfocused and inefficient allocator of capital. Silver Point and Elliott, in conjunction with the Board and post-emergence management team, made strong capital allocation at New Delphi a priority. Investors that were paying attention could have deduced this from the new Directors' backgrounds and their strong alignment with the value-oriented shareholder base.

As a result, we assumed annual buybacks scaling from $250 million to $750 million throughout the projection period. Assuming 25% annual share price appreciation, diluted shares decline from 328 million in 2011 to 284 million by 2016E. This led to a roughly 15% EPS growth CAGR and 19% for FCF/S over the 5-year projection period (see Exhibit 3.11).

Key Takeaways

- *Understand what the company does and how it makes money*

- *Focus on the two or three core drivers of the company's business*

- *Business due diligence seeks to verify a company's competitive position and the resilience of its business model, a.k.a. its "moat"*

- *Differentiated products, intellectual property, scale, brand, customer relationships, pricing power, and high upfront capital investment all support a company's moat*

- *Financial due diligence explores historical performance, primarily as a prologue for the future—visualize what the company will look like over the next one, two, five, or even ten years*

- *Equity investors ignore balance sheet and capital structure at their own peril*

- *Efficient capital allocation is a key differentiator for best-in-class companies*

- *The most prevalent ways to deploy capital include: organic growth projects, M&A, buybacks, dividends, and debt paydown*

Chapter Four

Step IV:
Valuation & Catalysts

What's the stock worth?

By now, you know how to analyze a company's business model and how it makes money. You also know how to measure financial performance. Now it's time to dig in on valuation. This sequencing is important. How can you value a company without first understanding the business and its underlying financials?

Our first book, *Investment Banking*, provides a 400-page, 100,000-word overview of valuation. This chapter captures the most critical concepts in a fraction of the space.

Your valuation work needs to address two key questions. First, what is the company worth? Second, how does that compare to its public market valuation? In other words, is the stock attractive at the current price? Your returns depend on paying the right price at the right time—avoid the trap of "*good company, bad stock.*"

Our valuation discussion starts with the basics. The essential Wall Street toolkit includes a mix of market, intrinsic, and M&A-based valuations. We also cover some of the more nuanced tools including sum-of-the-parts and net asset value.

Other approaches to valuation are less technical and more event-driven. So-called "catalysts" have the potential to drive meaningful share price appreciation. They may be internally-driven as part of an evolving management strategy or external, such as shareholder activism.

A combination of the above-mentioned valuation tools is used to determine your price target (PT) for a given stock. The PT is a core component of the final investment decision, whether *buy, short, track,* or *pass.* Without it, you cannot properly quantify the upside potential and risk/reward trade-off.

Valuation

In the pages that follow, we detail the key valuation tools used for stock picking (see Exhibit 4.1).

EXHIBIT 4.1 Valuation

Valuation

  I. Market and Intrinsic Valuation

       a. Comparable Companies

       b. Discounted Cash Flow

       c. Sum-of-the-Parts

       d. Net Asset Value

 II. Buyout Valuation

       a. Precedent Transactions

       b. Leveraged Buyout Analysis

       c. Accretion / (Dilution)

Market and Intrinsic Valuation

As outlined in Step II, *comparable companies analysis* ("comps") lies at the heart of valuation. Key trading multiples for a company are calculated and compared to peers. This relative analysis helps identify whether a stock may be mispriced and represents a buying opportunity.

A more academic tool is *discounted cash flow analysis* (DCF), which values a company based on the FCF it is expected to generate in perpetuity. These cash flows, however, need to be discounted to the present. In essence, the multiples-based approach to valuation is shorthand for a DCF. The multiples are meant to capture the present value (PV) of the company's future cash flows.

There are several variations on the valuation approaches discussed above. For example, a *sum-of-the-parts* (SOTP) approach may be appropriate for companies with diverse business segments. SOTP values each segment separately using one or more of the techniques listed above. The values of the individual pieces are then summed.

Net asset value analysis (NAV) is similar to SOTP. It is typically used for companies that house multiple financial or physical assets under one umbrella. The analysis relies upon summing the market value of these holdings, less the company's liabilities.

Comparable Companies

For publicly-traded companies, the market has already established a valuation mark. Their shares trade on a public exchange where investors buy and sell them at a given price. Your job is to determine whether those shares are fairly priced, undervalued, or overvalued.

Comps is built upon the premise that public peers provide a natural reference point for valuation. This, of course, assumes that the market is properly valuing these companies. The first step is finding the right peer set. For some companies, this exercise is relatively simple. A large U.S. food and beverage company would naturally be compared to Coca-Cola (KO), General Mills (GIS), Kellogg (K), Kraft Heinz (KHC), and PepsiCo (PEP). For others, the exercise requires more creativity as there are no clear peers.

The peer companies are then *benchmarked* against one another based on metrics such as size, growth, profitability, returns, and credit quality. Sector-specific criteria are also added as appropriate. Their relative ranking provides clues as to why certain companies trade at a premium or discount to the group. Valuation is then framed accordingly.

In Exhibit 4.2, we benchmark Delphi vs. its peers. By now, detailed work on Delphi's business model and competitors enabled us to expand and refine the set of peer companies. We dissected them into groups of *secular growers* and *production-linked* auto suppliers. The constituents of each group are shown in Exhibit 4.3, where we display Delphi's detailed comps output page.

Trading multiples are at the core of comps, most notably EV/EBITDA, P/E, and P/FCF (or the inverse, FCF yield). Higher multiples are typically tied to higher performance and expectations. The savvy investor looks for a breakdown in these correlations. Perhaps the market is misreading growth prospects, cost-cutting initiatives, capital return opportunities, or other key catalysts. Your job is to assess whether the discrepancy represents an attractive opportunity.

Most of the time, the valuation disconnect is entirely justified. This is particularly true for so-called value traps. They have fundamental or structural problems that threaten to depress future earnings. So, a 15x multiple today may actually be 25x based on lower future earnings. As a close friend of ours likes to say: "Everything looks cheap as it's going to zero."

Sometimes, however, you strike gold. The valuation discount jumps off the page—e.g., the company's growth rates are top quartile, but valuation multiples lag peers. In most cases, more nuanced analysis is needed. Otherwise, the market likely would have eliminated the arbitrage long ago.

EXHIBIT 4.2 Benchmarking Analysis

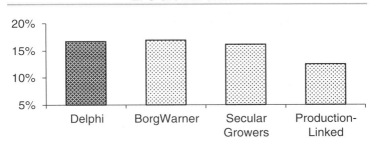

EPS Growth CAGR

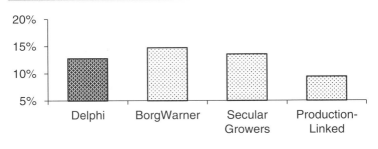

EBITDA Margins

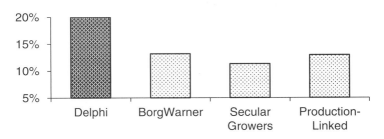

Return on Invested Capital (ROIC)

Now let's explore Delphi. Per Exhibit 4.2, its EPS growth CAGR was comfortably above production-linked comps and largely in line with the secular growers, albeit slightly below best-in-class BorgWarner. Its 12.7% EBITDA margin was also higher than production-linked players at 9.5% and approaching those of the secular growers. Further, Delphi's 20.5% ROIC was substantially higher than both peer category means.

Yet, as shown in Exhibit 4.3, Delphi traded at a significant discount to the secular growers peer set by all valuation measures—EV/EBITDA, P/E, and FCF yield. Its 2013E EV/EBITDA of 3.5x and P/E of 5x were relatively in line with the production-linked players, but multiple turns lower than secular growers who averaged approximately 6x and 11x, respectively.

Skepticism around the sustainability of Delphi's low tax rate from its UK incorporation likely helped fuel the P/E discount. In other words, investors were applying a haircut to future tax savings, thereby lowering their EPS estimates. This also manifested itself in Delphi's 15% 2013E FCF yield, which was markedly cheaper than the means of both groups. This was despite management's best efforts to highlight the sustainability of the company's tax benefits on the IPO roadshow and ensuing earnings calls.

In sum, Delphi shared a similar financial profile to the secular growers but was being valued like a production-linked player. The market was clearly skeptical of New Delphi's performance on a go-forward basis. Our work in Step III, however, gave us confidence that the new business model was working. With time and sustained performance, we believed the bankruptcy taint would dissipate and Delphi would re-rate higher.

EXHIBIT 4.3 Comparable Companies Analysis—Trading Multiples Output Page

($ in millions, except share price)

Comparable Companies Analysis

Company	Ticker	Current Share Price	% of 52-wk High	Equity Value	Enterprise Value	EV / EBITDA			P / E			FCF Yield		
						'11E	'12E	'13E	'11E	'12E	'13E	'11E	'12E	'13E
Secular Growers														
Autoliv	ALV	$52.90	63%	$4,962	$5,048	4.3x	4.2x	4.0x	7.9x	7.9x	7.6x	8.6%	9.6%	9.8%
BorgWarner	BWA	$65.63	80%	$8,451	$9,527	9.0x	7.8x	6.8x	15.1x	13.1x	11.0x	3.9%	5.9%	7.2%
Gentex	GNTX	$28.18	84%	$4,067	$3,611	12.9x	11.0x	9.5x	24.3x	20.1x	17.1x	2.0%	3.7%	5.6%
Harman	HAR	$40.77	79%	$2,931	$2,624	6.8x	6.0x	5.3x	16.3x	13.5x	11.9x	8.1%	8.2%	8.2%
Johnson Controls	JCI	$32.45	90%	$22,101	$24,957	8.3x	6.7x	5.8x	12.4x	10.2x	8.4x	1.0%	5.0%	7.0%
Visteon	VC	$57.43	76%	$2,985	$3,487	5.2x	4.6x	4.2x	15.5x	12.0x	10.5x	–	5.5%	7.5%
Delphi	**DLPH**	**$22.00**	**NA**	**$7,221**	**$8,501**	**4.2x**	**3.9x**	**3.5x**	**6.7x**	**6.0x**	**5.0x**	**10.1%**	**12.5%**	**14.8%**
Mean						**7.7x**	**6.7x**	**5.9x**	**15.2x**	**12.8x**	**11.1x**	**4.7%**	**6.3%**	**7.5%**
Production-Linked														
American Axle	AXL	$8.70	54%	$656	$1,592	4.3x	4.0x	3.6x	4.3x	4.2x	3.6x	3.2%	8.6%	13.1%
Dana	DAN	$13.33	70%	$2,863	$3,721	5.1x	4.5x	4.0x	8.5x	7.6x	6.0x	6.0%	9.7%	11.9%
Lear	LEA	$41.81	75%	$4,480	$3,616	3.5x	3.2x	3.0x	7.8x	7.4x	6.9x	5.8%	10.9%	11.4%
Magna	MGA	$34.06	55%	$8,260	$7,127	3.7x	3.5x	3.1x	8.7x	7.7x	6.5x	9.9%	8.6%	10.5%
Tenneco	TEN	$29.15	63%	$1,800	$2,988	5.1x	4.3x	3.8x	10.9x	8.4x	7.0x	4.2%	9.7%	11.3%
TRW	TRW	$34.18	55%	$4,570	$5,407	3.2x	3.1x	2.9x	4.9x	4.9x	4.8x	12.0%	12.8%	14.6%
Delphi	**DLPH**	**$22.00**	**NA**	**$7,221**	**$8,501**	**4.2x**	**3.9x**	**3.5x**	**6.7x**	**6.0x**	**5.0x**	**10.1%**	**12.5%**	**14.8%**
Mean						**4.1x**	**3.7x**	**3.4x**	**7.5x**	**6.7x**	**5.8x**	**6.9%**	**10.1%**	**12.1%**

Discounted Cash Flow

The basic premise of a DCF is that a company should be worth the present value of its future cash flows. This is known as *intrinsic value* given its basis in the underlying cash flows of a business. In this sense, the DCF serves as a helpful check on market-based approaches such as comps, which may be distorted during overly exuberant or bearish periods. It is also valuable when there are limited (or no) pure play peer companies.

In theory, a DCF should be the most accurate way to value a company. In practice, however, there are key considerations that limit its relevance and reliability. Most notably, it is highly dependent on assumptions regarding future FCF projections, which are inherently uncertain. Their uncertainty increases the farther out you go in the projection period. Additional assumptions regarding *discount rate* and *terminal value* further cloud the picture. As a result, the DCF valuation is viewed in terms of a range that is sensitized for key inputs, most notably discount rate and *exit multiple*.

Exhibit 4.4 displays the DCF output for Delphi.

EXHIBIT 4.4 Delphi DCF Analysis Output Page

($ in millions, except per share data, fiscal year ending December 31)

DCF Analysis

	2011E	Year 1 2012E	Year 2 2013E	Year 3 2014E	Year 4 2015E	Year 5 2016E
EBITDA	$2,044	$2,157	$2,433	$2,731	$2,948	$3,172
Less: Depreciation & Amortization	(478)	(490)	(532)	(575)	(610)	(645)
EBIT	$1,567	$1,667	$1,901	$2,155	$2,338	$2,526
Less Taxes	(317)	(338)	(385)	(436)	(473)	(512)
Plus: Depreciation & Amortization	478	490	532	575	610	645
Less: Capital Expenditures	(629)	(747)	(811)	(878)	(931)	(985)
Less: Inc. / (Dec.) in Net Working Capital	(138)	(26)	(61)	(65)	(50)	(50)
Unlevered FCF	$959	$1,047	$1,175	$1,352	$1,494	$1,625
Discount Period (mid-year convention)		0.5	1.5	2.5	3.5	4.5
Discount Factor @ 10% WACC		0.95	0.87	0.79	0.72	0.65
Present Value of FCF		$998	$1,019	$1,065	$1,070	$1,058

Enterprise Value		
Cumulative Present Value of FCF	$5,210	A

Terminal Value		
Terminal Year EBITDA	$3,172	
Exit Multiple	5.0x	
Terminal Value	$15,860	
Discount Factor	0.62	
Present Value of Terminal Value	$9,848	B
% of Enterprise Value	65%	

Enterprise Value (A + B)	$15,058	C

Implied Equity Value and Share Price	
Enterprise Value	$15,058
Less: Total Debt	(2,173)
Less: Preferred Stock	-
Less: Noncontrolling Interest	(462)
Plus: Cash and Cash Equivalents	1,355
Implied Equity Value	$13,778
Fully Diluted Shares	328
Implied Share Price	$41.97

FCF Projections A DCF is typically based on a five-year forecast, enough to carry a company through a business cycle and reach a theoretical steady state.[1] The projections begin with sales or EBITDA and cascade down to *unlevered FCF*, or FCF before deducting interest expense. They are derived from management guidance (if provided), equity research, and third-party sources. Ultimately, you need to rely on your own company- and sector-specific diligence and judgment. The Delphi projections developed in Step III serve as the backbone for our DCF.

Terminal Value Given the difficulties in projecting a company's financials in perpetuity, a terminal value is used to capture cash flows beyond the five-year forecast.

The terminal value is typically calculated on the basis of a multiple of the company's *terminal year*[2] EBITDA. This is also known as the *exit multiple method* (EMM).[3] Standard practice for most sectors is to use the EV/EBITDA multiple for comparable companies (see Exhibit 4.5). For Delphi, we assumed an exit multiple of 5x, which was a blended average of the secular

---

[1] The projection period may be longer depending on the company's sector, stage of development, and underlying predictability of its financial performance.

[2] Terminal year refers to the final year of the projection period.

[3] An alternative approach is the *perpetuity growth method*, which calculates terminal value by growing a company's terminal year FCF in perpetuity at a sustainable long-term rate.

growers and production-linked peer sets, weighted towards the latter for conservatism.

EXHIBIT 4.5 Exit Multiple Method

$$EBITDA_n \times \text{ Exit Multiple}$$

where: n = terminal year of the projection period

Weighted Average Cost of Capital (WACC) represents the rate used to discount a company's projected FCF and terminal value to the present. It is the "weighted average" of the required return on invested capital in the company, both debt and equity. WACC is commonly referred to as discount rate or *cost of capital.*

As shown in Exhibit 4.6, the WACC calculation requires several baseline assumptions.

EXHIBIT 4.6 Calculation of WACC

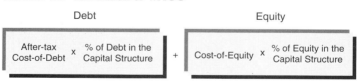

The percentage mix of debt and equity is based on an assumed long-term capital structure for the company. A typical mix might be 30% debt, 70% equity. In the absence of specific company guidance, look at its historical capital structure and that of peers.

Cost-of-debt is typically gleaned from the yield on a company's bonds. Depending on the interest rate environment, high-quality investment grade companies have yields in the low/mid-single-digits, while high yield bonds may feature coupons several hundred basis points higher. More speculative bonds yield north of 10%.

Cost-of-equity is more difficult to gauge. Pros use the capital asset pricing model (CAPM),[4] a formula designed to capture the expected rate of return on a company's equity. Since inception, the S&P 500 has returned roughly 11% on average, including dividends. As with debt, cost-of-equity is higher for riskier companies, and lower for more stable ones.

In the low interest rate environment of the post-Great Recession era, a typical WACC was in the 7% to 12% range for most companies. Large-cap investment grade companies gravitated towards the lower end, or even below. More speculative companies were at the high end of the range, or greater.

For Delphi in 2011, we calculated a WACC of 10%. This relied on a 6% cost-of-debt (4.8% after-tax) based on

---

[4]CAPM = risk-free rate + beta × market risk premium. *Risk-free rate* is the expected yield on a "riskless" security, typically a 10-year U.S. Treasury Note. *Beta* measures the covariance between the return on a company's stock and the stock market. Higher beta stocks are more volatile. *Market risk premium* represents the incremental return over the risk-free rate that equity investors expect to earn, typically ranging from 5% to 8%.

its benchmark bond yield and a 12.5% cost-of-equity. We also assumed a long-term debt-to-total capitalization mix of 30%, implying 70% equity.

Present Value Calculating PV centers on the notion that a dollar today is worth more than a dollar tomorrow, known as the *time value of money*. This is because a dollar generates returns over time through investments and earned interest.

For a DCF, PV is calculated by multiplying the annual FCF and terminal value by their respective *discount factors*. A discount factor is the fractional value representing the PV of one dollar received at a future date, given an assumed discount rate. At a 10% WACC, the discount factor for one dollar received at the end of Year 1 is 0.91 $(1/(1+10\%)^{\wedge}1)$. Therefore, the PV of $100 million of FCF produced in Year 1 is $91 million.

In practice, the PV calculation is adjusted to reflect the reality that FCF is generated throughout the year rather than at year-end. This is known as *mid-year convention*. Using mid-year convention and a 10% WACC, the discount factor for Year 1 would be 0.95 $(1/(1+10\%)^{\wedge}0.5)$. As shown in Exhibit 4.4, we used the mid-year approach for the Delphi DCF. For the terminal value, however, we used the full-year discount approach given the lump sum amount is assumed to be received at the end of the projection period. Note that the discount factor here is 0.62 vs. 0.65 for Year 5 FCF.

Putting It All Together

Enterprise Value The company's five years of projected FCF and terminal value are discounted to the present. The sum of these values represents enterprise value. For Delphi, the PV of five years of projected FCF summed to $5.2 billion (see "A" in Exhibit 4.4). The terminal year EBITDA of $3.2 billion was capitalized at a 5x exit multiple to provide a terminal value of $15.9 billion. This value was then discounted at a 10% WACC to its PV of $9.8 billion (see "B"). The PV of the future FCF and terminal value summed to an enterprise value of $15.1 billion (see "C").

Equity Value is an easy calculation once you know enterprise value. Just subtract net debt, preferred stock, and noncontrolling interest. For Delphi, net debt of $818 million and noncontrolling interest of $462 million were subtracted from enterprise value of $15.1 billion to provide an implied equity value of $13.8 billion.

Share Price Next, you divide implied equity value by fully diluted shares. For Delphi, $13.8 billion of equity value was divided by 328 million diluted shares to yield a share price of nearly $42. This represented over 90% upside to the IPO share price of $22.

Sensitivity Analysis Given the multiple assumptions discussed above, the DCF valuation is viewed in terms of a range rather than a single value. This range is driven by sensitizing key inputs, such as WACC and exit multiple. Financial performance drivers may also be sensitized, most notably sales growth rates and profit margins. This so-called *sensitivity analysis* is a testament to the notion that valuation is as much "art as science."

As shown in Exhibit 4.7, a half turn change in exit multiple equates to $3 per share of value. Likewise, a 0.5% change in WACC affects implied share price by roughly $0.75.

EXHIBIT 4.7 DCF Sensitivity Analysis

		Implied Share Price			
			Exit Multiple		
		4.0x	4.5x	5.0x	5.5x	6.0x
WACC	9.0%	$37	$41	$44	$47	$50
	9.5%	$37	$40	$43	$46	$49
	10.0%	$36	$39	$42	$45	$48
	10.5%	$35	$38	$41	$44	$47
	11.0%	$35	$37	$40	$43	$46

Sum-of-the-Parts

Some companies fall under the category of pure plays. Their business model is focused and relatively easy to label. The Home Depot (HD) and McDonald's (MCD) come to mind. On the other end of the spectrum are conglomerates, where a group of largely unrelated businesses are housed under one corporate umbrella.

Many companies fall somewhere in between. They have multiple business segments that may share similar inputs, materials, customers, and end markets, but with different growth and margin profiles. For these companies, it is often helpful to perform a SOTP that values each of the segments separately.

SOTP enables you to determine whether there is a valuation arbitrage between the whole and its parts. In some cases, you may find that the parts are worth meaningfully more than where the consolidated business is trading. This may signal a buying opportunity given the market's misinterpretation of the embedded value of certain segments. The spin-off or divestiture of one or more of these segments can serve as a catalyst to unlock this value.

A standard SOTP employs a comps approach to valuation. You find the best peers for each segment and then apply their multiples accordingly. This is the natural approach for valuing a division that is being contemplated for a spin-off. The values for each segment are then summed to arrive at an implied valuation for the entire company.

A "mix-and-match" approach may also apply for SOTP. For example, your thesis may be for one or more segments to be sold. In this case, precedent transactions or leveraged buyout ("LBO") analysis can be used to value those pieces.

While SOTP wasn't particularly relevant for Delphi at its IPO, it did apply to Rockwood Holdings (ROC). In 2011, ROC was a leading global specialty chemicals company with four diverse business segments. As shown in Exhibit 4.8, ROC's SOTP at year-end 2011 yielded a $60 implied share price. This represented over 50% upside to its $39.37 share price at the time.

Over the next two years, Rockwood proceeded to sell its Advanced Ceramics and Titanium Dioxide businesses, as well as part of its Performance Additives segment. Then, in July 2014, the remainder of ROC was sold to Albemarle (ALB) for nearly $80 per share. All told, ROC shareholders doubled their money from December 2011. Clearly, the SOTP signaled embedded value that wasn't being recognized by the market.

EXHIBIT 4.8 Rockwood Sum-of-the-Parts

Rockwood Holdings (ROC)
Sum-of-the-Parts (SOTP)

($ in millions, except per share data)

	2012E EBITDA	Target EV/EBITDA Multiple	Implied Enterprise Value	% Total
Segments				
Specialty Chemicals	$350	8.5x	$2,975	44%
Performance Additives	165	8.0x	1,320	19%
Titanium Dioxide	175	5.0x	875	13%
Advanced Ceramics	185	9.0x	1,665	24%
Total Segment EBITDA	**$875**	**7.8x**	**$6,835**	**100%**
Less: Corporate	(45)	7.8x	(352)	
Total Consolidated EBITDA	**$830**	**7.8x**	**$6,483**	
Less: Debt			(1,729)	
Less: Noncontrolling Interest			(311)	
Plus: Cash			358	
Implied Equity Value			**$4,801**	
Diluted Shares			80	
Implied Share Price			**$60.00**	
Share Price a/o 12/30/2011			$39.37	
% Upside			*52%*	

Net Asset Value

NAV analysis is traditionally used for businesses that house multiple distinct financial or physical assets. Common examples include Real Estate Investment Trusts (REITs), oil & gas exploration and production (E&P) companies, and financial holding companies.

NAV is meant to reflect the market value of a company's assets, less its liabilities. For holding companies with stakes in multiple businesses, there may be a disconnect between the parent company's share price and the market value of its holdings.

Liberty Media (formerly, LMCA), which owned stakes in several public and private companies, is a classic example. Per Exhibit 4.9, in December 2012, LMCA's $105.56 share price represented an 11% discount to the sum value of its holdings at market value. Contributing factors included complexity, embedded taxable gains, tight trading liquidity, and ironically, uncertainty about how to collapse the public discount to NAV. Ultimately, the spin-offs of core assets Starz Entertainment, the Atlanta Braves, and the Sirius XM equity stake created substantial value for Liberty shareholders. Those who held on were rewarded with a 15% annualized return through 2019.

There also may be a disconnect between market value and stated book value for a collection of assets. This is often due to depreciation for accounting purposes vs. the asset's actual useful life, as well as the net effects of dividends and buybacks.

Liquidation value analysis, which is often employed in distressed or bankruptcy scenarios, is a variant of NAV. It seeks to calculate the selling price of a firm's assets under a liquidation or forced sale scenario. If the liquidation value is greater than the sum of the company's liabilities, then the remaining value is available for equity holders. Given the dynamics of a forced sale, liquidation analysis applies meaningful discounts to the market value of assets.

EXHIBIT 4.9 Liberty Media Net Asset Value

Liberty Media (LMCA)
Net Asset Value (NAV)

($ in millions, except per share data)							As of 12/4/2012
	Ticker	% Owned	Shares Held	Share Price	Value	NAV per Share	% of NAV
Consolidated Assets							
Starz Entertainment		100%			$2,150	$17.24	15%
Atlanta Braves (MLB)		100%			550	4.41	4%
True Position		100%			200	1.60	1%
Other					350	2.81	2%
Total					**$3,250**	**$26.06**	**22%**
Publicly-Traded Securities							
Sirius XM	SIRI	50%	3,248.7	$2.76	$8,966	$71.90	61%
Live Nation	LYV	26%	48.7	8.77	427	3.43	3%
Time Warner Inc.	TWX	1%	9.4	44.77	421	3.37	3%
Time Warner Cable	TWC	1%	2.4	94.97	228	1.83	2%
Viacom	VIAB	1%	5.0	51.30	256	2.06	2%
Other					476	3.82	3%
Total					**$10,775**	**$86.40**	**73%**
Capital Structure							
Debt					($540)	($4.33)	(4%)
Cash & Equivalents					1,025	8.22	7%
Other					300	2.41	2%
Total					**$785**	**$6.30**	**5%**
Net Asset Value					**$14,810**		**100%**
Diluted Shares					125		
NAV per Share					**$118.76**		
Current Share Price					$105.56		
Premium / (Discount) to NAV					*(11.1%)*		

Buyout Valuation

Investors also examine valuation within a buyout or M&A context. They evaluate what a strategic buyer could pay for the company, often with specific acquirers in mind. They may also explore what a PE buyer can afford to pay for the business. Buyout valuation is particularly relevant for companies or sectors in play, where M&A is part of the investment thesis.

Key buyout valuation techniques include *precedent transactions analysis* ("precedents") and *LBO analysis*. Precedents derives valuation from multiples paid for comparable companies in prior transactions. LBO analysis examines the price a PE firm could pay for a given company and meet required return thresholds. For public acquirers, *accretion / (dilution) analysis* is also critical as it measures the pro forma effects of a transaction on EPS.

In theory, Delphi's modest valuation and low leverage post-IPO made a potential takeover feasible. In practice, however, the company's owners weren't in a hurry to sell given their perceived upside in the stock. Further, potential buyers were less likely to make aggressive M&A moves so soon after the Great Recession. More likely was an M&A scenario where Delphi would continue to upgrade the portfolio. This might include the sale of non-core businesses, or acquisitions to bolt on to its higher quality segments.

Precedent Transactions

Precedents, like comps, employs a multiples-based approach to valuation. The multiples used, however, are those paid for similar companies in past M&A transactions. As with comps, they are displayed in a format that allows for easy comparison and benchmarking.

Finding the right group of comparable acquisitions is the foundation for precedents. Like comps, the best comparable acquisitions involve companies similar to the target on a fundamental level. As a general rule, more recent transactions—those that have occurred within the past three years or so—are the most relevant.

Exhibit 4.10 displays auto supplier M&A transactions that were announced between 2009 and 2011. Given the global recession and muted M&A activity, there were few sizable large transactions and only one public company deal. The average EBITDA multiple paid was 6.5x, and 6x when adjusting for announced synergies. Synergies refer to the financial and strategic benefits that result from a combination, typically cost savings and revenue growth opportunities. These multiples were somewhat depressed vs. historical precedents given the time period, which straddled the Great Recession.

EXHIBIT 4.10 Precedent Transactions Output Page

($ in millions)

Precedent Transactions Analysis								
Date	**Acquirer /**	**Transaction**	**Purchase**	**Enterprise**	**EV / EBITDA**		**EBITDA**
Announced	**Target**	**Type**	**Consideration**	**Value**	**Actual**	**w/Synergies**	**Margin**
7/28/11	GKN plc / Getrag - Axle Business	Public / Private	Cash	$482	5.6x	-	13%
7/28/11	Sterling Group / Stackpole Ltd	LBO / Private	Cash	$285	5.7x	-	17%
4/8/11	The Gores Group / Sage Auto Interiors	LBO / Private	Cash	$140	5.0x	-	12%
12/17/10	BorgWarner / Haldex Traction Systems	Public / Private	Cash	$205	8.3x	-	15%
10/15/10	Carlisle Companies / Hawk Corporation	Public / Public	Cash	$410	7.3x	6.2x	20%
12/16/09	Metalsa, S.A. de C.V. / Dana - Structural Products	Private / Public Sub.	Cash	$147	6.8x	-	6%
11/2/09	Faurecia / EMCON Technologies	Public / Private	Stock	$408	7.0x	5.8x	2%
Mean					**6.5x**	**6.0x**	**12%**
Median					**6.8x**	**6.0x**	**13%**

Under normal market conditions, multiples for precedents tend to be higher than those for comps for two principal reasons. First, buyers generally pay a "control premium" when purchasing another company. This premium is typically in the 30% to 40% range, although it can be significantly higher. In return, the acquirer receives control over the target's business and future cash flows. Second, strategic buyers often realize synergies that support a higher purchase price.

Once you identify the best comparable acquisitions, you dig in on the specific circumstances and context for each deal. This enables you to better interpret the multiple paid and its relevance to your stock. Many factors affect the multiples for a given deal. Among these are the macro and capital markets environment at the time of the transaction, sale process dynamics, synergies, and whether the buyer was strategic or PE.

Buyer and seller motivations, including friendly vs. hostile situations, as well as the purchase consideration (i.e., mix of cash and stock paid to target shareholders) are also relevant. Typically, all-cash deals have higher premiums paid than stock deals. By receiving cash upfront, selling shareholders are compensated for bypassing the opportunity to participate in any future upside of the combined company.

Key Transaction Multiples

EV/EBITDA multiples are at the core of precedents with enterprise value based on offer price per share rather than current share price. As noted above, offer price typically reflects a significant premium to current share price. For particular sectors, such as banks, P/E and P/B multiples may be more relevant.

Investors often look at transaction multiples adjusted for expected synergies. This approach adds synergies to the target's standalone EBITDA, which serves to decrease the implied multiple paid and highlight the buyer's perspective (see Exhibit 4.11).

EXHIBIT 4.11 Synergies-Adjusted EV/EBITDA Calculation

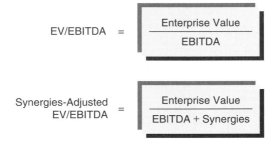

Leveraged Buyout Analysis

An LBO is the acquisition of a company using a sizable amount of debt to finance the purchase price, typically 60% to 70%. The remaining portion is funded with an equity contribution by a PE firm.

LBO analysis is used by PE investors to assess valuation for potential targets. Stock market investors need to understand how PE investors frame valuation to determine whether a given public company may be a target (a.k.a., a "take-private" candidate). In many cases, the implied LBO price serves as a floor valuation on a stock. This is also informative for assessing short positions given the inherent take-out risk for underperforming companies.

In practice, most publicly-traded companies are not viable take-private candidates. Any combination of size, price, business profile, ability to support high leverage, and actionability serve as potential impediments. Delphi's LBO viability was mixed. While its lagging valuation was attractive for suitors, its size, checkered past, and cyclicality were deterrents. Moreover, the 2011 market was still adjusting to the post-Great Recession world. So, the prospect of re-leveraging a recently bankrupt auto supplier was not top of mind for PE investors and financing sources.

Like the DCF, LBO analysis is based on a five-year projection model. However, there are additional complexities, including assumptions for purchase price, *financing structure, debt terms,* and exit multiple.

LBO leverage typically ranges from 4.5x to 6.5x debt-to-EBITDA depending on credit quality, sector, size, and market conditions. The structure and cost-of-debt also depend on these factors. For example, a more speculative cyclical business would have lower leverage and a higher blended cost-of-debt than a more established subscription-based business. The debt component is supported by a minimum equity contribution, typically at least 25% of the purchase price.

The exit multiple for LBO analysis is based on where comps trade on a mid-cycle or normalized basis.[5] Once the cornerstone LBO assumptions are in place, you can solve for a purchase price that satisfies PE returns. PE firms typically target annualized returns (internal rate of return, or "IRR") in the mid-teens and higher, or a 2x cash-on-cash ("CoC") return upon exit within five years. The exit takes place via a sale or IPO.

---

[5] For conservatism, the exit multiple is generally assumed to be at, or below, the entry multiple.

How Do LBOs Generate Returns?

LBOs generate returns through a combination of debt repayment and enterprise value growth. Regarding the former, assuming a constant EV/EBITDA multiple, a $1 decrease in debt increases equity value by $1. Per the latter, enterprise value growth may be a function of higher EBITDA or multiple expansion. In Exhibit 4.12, we illustrate how this works, including the IRR and CoC calculations. Let's assume the following:

I. PE firm purchases a company for $1 billion, or 10x $100 million of EBITDA

II. Acquisition is financed with 65% debt ($650 million) and 35% equity ($350 million), or 6.5x leverage

III. Company produces $50 million of annual FCF for five years ($250 million cumulative), which is used to repay debt

IV. Company is sold for $1.5 billion at end of Year 5 (assuming constant 10x exit multiple on Year 5 EBITDA of $150 million)

EXHIBIT 4.12 How LBOs Generate Returns

($ in millions)

	Year 0	Year 1	Year 2	Year 3	Year 4	Year 5
Initial Equity Contribution and Calculation of Equity Value at Exit						
Equity Contribution						
	($350)					
Total Debt, beginning balance		$650	$600	$550	$500	$450
Free Cash Flow		(50)	(50)	(50)	(50)	(50)
Total Debt, ending balance		**$650**	**$600**	**$550**	**$450**	**$400**
Sale Price						$1,500
Less: Ending Debt Balance						(400)
Equity Value at Exit						**$1,100**

= Beginning Debt Balance$_{year\ 1}$ – FCF$_{year\ 1}$
= $650 million – $50 million

IRR Timeline and Calculation

	Year 0	Year 1	Year 2	Year 3	Year 4	Year 5
Initial Equity Investment	($350)					
Dividends / (Investment)	-	-	-	-	-	-
Equity Value at Exit		-	-	-	-	$1,100
Total Cash Inflows / (Outflows)	**($350)**	**-**	**-**	**-**	**-**	**$1,100**

= IRR (Initial Equity Investment : Equity Value at Exit)
= IRR (–$350 million : $1,100 million)

Internal Rate of Return (IRR)	**25.7%**
Cash-on-Cash Return (CoC)	**3.1x**

= Cash Inflows / Cash Outflows
= $1,100 million / $350 million

[202]

After five years, the $650 million of initial debt has shrunk to $400 million as $50 million FCF per year has gone to repay debt. Given the $1.5 billion sale price and $400 million of remaining debt, the PE firm receives $1.1 billion of cash upon exit. Based on the $350 million initial equity contribution, the IRR is 25.7% (using the MS Excel IRR function) and CoC return is 3.1x.

Accretion / (Dilution)

Accretion / (dilution) analysis is critical for examining M&A-related stock opportunities. It measures the pro forma effects of a transaction on the acquirer's EPS using a given financing structure. If the PF EPS is higher than the acquirer's pre-deal EPS, the transaction is said to be *accretive*. Conversely, if the PF EPS is lower, the transaction is *dilutive*.

Yes, the headline price paid for the target is important, as is the multiple. But, investors' first question tends to be whether the deal is accretive and by how much. Dilutive transactions lower EPS or FCF/S, thereby reducing shareholder value (assuming a constant multiple). Consequently, acquirers shy away from dilutive transactions.

So, how does the math work? A rule of thumb for 100% stock transactions is that when an acquirer purchases a target with a lower P/E, the acquisition is accretive. This is intuitive. When a company pays a lower multiple for the target's earnings than the multiple at which its own earnings trade, it mathematically has to be accretive.

Conversely, all-stock transactions where an acquirer purchases a higher P/E target are *de facto* dilutive. Sizable synergies, however, may serve to offset this convention. Furthermore, if the transaction is largely debt-financed, the target's net income contribution often outweighs the associated incremental interest expense, resulting in accretion. Investors look for acquirers to maximize accretion by showing purchase price discipline, sourcing the optimal financing, and identifying significant achievable synergies.

Exhibit 4.13 displays a graphical depiction of an illustrative accretion / (dilution) calculation with a comparison of 100% cash (debt-financed), 50% cash / 50% stock, and 100% stock financing.

EXHIBIT 4.13 Accretion / (Dilution) Analysis

($ in millions, except per share data)

Accretion / (Dilution) Analysis

Target Assumptions

Offer Price per Share	$25.00
Current Share Price	$18.50
% premium	*35%*
Diluted Shares	200
Purchase of TargetCo Equity	**$5,000**
TargetCo EBIT	$350
Synergies	$50

Acquirer Assumptions

BuyerCo Share Price	$50.00
BuyerCo Cost-of-Debt	6.0%
BuyerCo Tax Rate	25%

	100% Cash	50% Cash / 50% Stock	100% Stock
Cash	$5,000	$2,500	-
Stock	-	$2,500	$5,000
BuyerCo EBIT	$1,000	$1,000	$1,000
TargetCo EBIT	350	350	350
Synergies	50	50	50
PF EBIT	**$1,400**	**$1,400**	**$1,400**
Pre-deal Interest Exp.	(150)	(150)	(150)
Incremental Interest Exp.	(300)	(150)	-
Earnings Before Taxes	**$950**	**$1,100**	**$1,250**
Income Taxes @ 25%	(238)	(275)	(313)
PF Net Income	**$713**	**$825**	**$938**
Pre-deal Net Income	**$527**	**$527**	**$527**
Pre-deal Diluted Shares	100	100	100
Net New Shares Issued	-	50	100
PF Diluted Shares	**100**	**150**	**200**
PF Diluted EPS	$7.13	$5.50	$4.69
Pre-deal Diluted EPS	5.27	5.27	5.27
Accretion / (Dilution) - $	**$1.86**	**$0.23**	**($0.58)**
Accretion / (Dilution) - %	**35%**	**4%**	**(11%)**
Accretive / Dilutive	*Accretive*	*Accretive*	*Dilutive*

Catalysts

Catalysts are events with the potential to create shareholder value through higher earnings power, multiple expansion (a so-called "re-rating"), or both. The savvy investor seeks to anticipate catalysts and the expected market reaction. This means initiating a position before a catalyst is announced or reflected in the share price.

Once a catalyst occurs, you must differentiate between a one-time share price pop vs. a more fundamental revaluation and long-term earnings ramp. The one-time pop might be due to an unsustainable short-term earnings bump (e.g., competitor dislocation or weather). Such pops are likely to be transient, subject to reversal in the following months. A fundamental revaluation would be premised on a stronger foundation—strategic M&A, portfolio realignment, major cost-cutting, shareholder-friendly capital allocation, or a blockbuster new product.

Below, we discuss catalysts within the context of anticipating events that promise to unlock value (see Exhibit 4.14). This stands in contrast to Chapter 1, where we screened for corporate events *after* they were publicly announced.

EXHIBIT 4.14 Catalysts

Catalysts

- Earnings

- Investor Days

- Mergers & Acquisitions

- Spin-offs & Divestitures

- Restructurings & Turnarounds

- Buybacks & Dividends

- Refinancings

- Management Changes

- Shareholder Activism

- New Products & Customers

- Regulatory

The Delphi investment thesis involved numerous potential catalysts—namely, earnings acceleration, capital returns, portfolio pruning, acquisitions, and a fading bankruptcy taint. The promise of next-generation products was also on the horizon. Astute investors could have gained confidence around the architecture put in place by the lead shareholders during the bankruptcy process, and that the active, highly accomplished Board would pull the right levers for value creation. Some catalysts came to fruition, some didn't, and some were welcome surprises.

Earnings

Upon announcing earnings, a company's share price may move up or down significantly. Why? Shouldn't the market have anticipated the earnings results within a somewhat narrow band? In most cases, the company is basically the same just after announcing earnings as before. So, what justifies such big potential swings?

The answer is simple. Companies are continuously evolving and striving to succeed in a competitive environment. At the very least, they are charged with delivering on their existing strategy. Earnings are a confirmation (or repudiation) of that strategy. In some sense, they are a quarterly report card for the company. Simply meeting expectations should produce a muted reaction from investors, while solid outperformance should be rewarded. Failure to deliver should be met with a strong rebuke, especially if there appear to be longer-term structural problems.

Suffice to say that earnings outperformance is central to any thesis. Solid execution and sustained earnings growth may be all that is necessary for a stock to be a big winner over time. A foundation of earnings compounders often serves as the backbone of a traditional equity investor's portfolio.

As a stock picker, you need to be able to compare quarterly earnings with prior year periods and consensus analyst estimates. In Step V, we provide analytical templates to facilitate this critical task.

Delphi's Q4'11 earnings release on January 26, 2012 was a critical one. It was the company's first post-IPO earnings report and its first time providing guidance. For the fourth quarter, sales were $3.9 billion (+6.8% y/y[6]), roughly in line with Street estimates. However, Q4'11 EBITDA of $530 million (+55% y/y) and EPS of $0.88 (+287% y/y) were massive beats, demonstrating management's strong execution and cost-cutting flow-through.

For the full year 2011, Delphi reported sales of $16 billion, EBITDA of $2.1 billion, and EPS of $3.49. These were sizable improvements over 2010 and well above Street expectations. The stock responded favorably, finishing up 4.7% for the day.

---

[6] y/y = year-over-year.

Companies also use earnings announcements to give or update guidance (if provided). Updates can take the form of confirming existing guidance or making revisions, whether upward or downward. In some cases, companies provide long-term sales or earnings goals, e.g., a 5-year sales target of $10 billion and 15%+ EBITDA margins. *Typically, the guidance is more important than the actual earnings given the forward-looking nature of the equity markets.* New guidance or revisions are important catalysts. Even a relatively small change can produce a large swing in the share price.

Beyond guidance, earnings calls provide management with the opportunity to announce major corporate events, new business developments, and changes in strategy that may serve as catalysts themselves. This new information is quickly processed by the market, which makes an initial assessment—the share price pops, drops, or remains largely unchanged. These new initiatives are then tracked over time by investors with the company held accountable for delivering on them.

Investor Days

From time to time, companies hold investor days to tell their in-depth story directly to current and prospective shareholders. These are typically large public events spanning several hours and can include product demos and facility tours (if held on site). They are led by the senior management team, often including division heads and business development executives. By the end of the investor day, attendees will have been presented with a comprehensive overview of the business and its strategic direction. A successful investor day can help reshape the company's narrative (if needed) and drive the share price higher.

Delphi held its first investor day in April 2012, only five months post-IPO. Going forward, the company elected to have an annual investor day to provide strategic updates, discuss capital allocation plans, announce acquisitions/new commercial endeavors, and provide guidance, as appropriate. In 2013, management laid out a plan to take EBITDA margins from under 14% to 16% by 2016. They also provided a long-term capital deployment plan earmarking 45% to 55% of operating cash flow for buybacks/acquisitions, 10% to 15% for dividends, and 35% to 40% for capex. The stock responded favorably, marching up 9.4% over the next two days.

Delphi's investor day in April 2016 was also noteworthy, setting forth goals for accelerated top line growth and EBITDA margins of 18.5% by 2020. Management also discussed the company's portfolio realignment strategy and announced the authorization of an additional $1.5 billion buyback. As with the 2013 event, Delphi's shares reacted positively, rising 6.7% over the following couple of days.

Mergers & Acquisitions

As discussed in Step I, various M&A scenarios can serve as meaningful catalysts. Event-driven investors and activists seek stocks where they anticipate M&A activity driving returns. This requires in-depth research on an industry to identify natural combinations, likely acquirers, and takeover candidates. Pay particular attention to sub-sectors where a recent takeover was done at a substantial premium. This often serves as a catalyst for peers to rally.

In May 2012, only six months after going public, Delphi announced the acquisition of FCI's Motorized Vehicles Division (MVL) for roughly $975 million. This represented 7x EBITDA and only 4.5x on a synergies-adjusted basis. Delphi's successful M&A execution was helped in no small part by Kevin Clark from the CFO seat. Clark had extensive M&A experience from his tenure at highly acquisitive Fisher Scientific—this proven skill set was fundamental to the Board's decision to recruit him to join Delphi in 2010.

MVL bolstered Delphi's already strong position in the high-growth, high-margin connectors market, while diversifying its customer base and expanding its Asia footprint. Financially, the transaction accelerated sales growth, enhanced overall margins, and was 5%+ accretive to EPS including synergies.

Delphi's share price rose 2.7% the day following transaction announcement and a further 5% the next trading day as the market absorbed the merits of the deal. By the end of 2012, the stock had increased nearly 38% since announcement date. Clearly, investors were pleased.

Three years later, in July 2015, Delphi was back at it again with the acquisition of public British cable management solutions provider HellermannTyton Group (LSE:HTY). The $1.85 billion purchase price represented 12.3x next twelve months EBITDA (9.1x synergies-adjusted) and a nearly 45% premium to HTY's prior day close. The high multiple paid reflected the strategic imperative behind the deal. HTY bolstered Delphi's already-strong position in electrical architecture, its largest segment. While the initial share price reaction was muted, the market eventually came around. By the end of 2015, Delphi's shares had risen 11% since deal announcement.

Along with the HellermannTyton deal, in 2015 Delphi disclosed several additional acquisitions/investments aimed at upgrading the technology in its product portfolio. It invested in a LiDAR sensing company, a software business focused on autonomous driving, and a tech company focused on fuel efficiency. Delphi was positioning itself at the forefront of autonomous driving, active safety, infotainment, and user experience.

Spin-offs & Divestitures

Investors often target companies with businesses or divisions they believe aren't being properly valued by the market. The basic premise is that the SOTP value of the two (or more) separate businesses is greater than the whole. In theory, separation should allow the market to assign a cleaner valuation to both the ParentCo and SpinCo, or DivestCo.

Ideally, you want to identify companies with potential spin-off or divestiture candidates early on. This enables you to participate in the upside upon announcement when the stock tends to pop. Many investors (including activists) specifically target these situations.

Part of the original Delphi investment thesis identified portfolio optimization as a potential catalyst, including the divestiture of non-core business segments. In this vein, in February 2015, the company announced the sale of its Thermal Systems segment to German auto supplier MAHLE for $727 million, or 9.5x EBITDA. Thermal had a lower growth and margin profile than Delphi as a whole. It also didn't fit with the company's increasing focus on secular growth areas. In the weeks leading up to announcement, Delphi's stock rose 9% as the deal was widely anticipated.

Two years later, Delphi executed another transaction, this one more transformative. In May 2017, it announced the tax-free spin-off of its Powertrain Systems segment, which was ultimately renamed Delphi Technologies and kept the DLPH ticker. ParentCo was renamed Aptiv (APTV, connoting knowledge, adaptiveness, and drive) and retained the higher-growth, higher-multiple Electrical/Electronic Architecture and Electronics & Safety segments. As such, Aptiv became a technology-focused pure play for investors concentrated on electrification and connected/autonomous vehicles. Meanwhile, Delphi Technologies would have a new management team and capital plan with the goal of reaccelerating top line growth and continuing to migrate up the value chain.

Upon spin announcement, the stock popped 11% and proceeded to advance 29% through year-end. Many sell-side research analysts had been assessing legacy Delphi on a SOTP basis for some time given the disparate growth and margin profile of its segments. Their analysis suggested that Delphi's parts were worth more than $100 per share, roughly 50% above the pre-announcement share price. Sure enough, the shares surpassed $100 before the spin closed in late 2017.

Restructurings & Turnarounds

Turnaround situations involve finding troubled companies with a viable path to redemption as the catalyst. Given the risks, your conviction in the revitalization strategy needs to be strong.

Delphi represented a classic turnaround. Its bloated cost structure, heavy debt load and legacy liabilities put the company into bankruptcy. This, in turn, led to underinvestment in the company's assets, which began to affect financial performance.

Under Chapter 11 bankruptcy protection, Delphi's Board and lead shareholders worked with CEO Rod O'Neal to devise a strategy to reinvent the company. This involved pruning the portfolio, removing burdensome UAW contracts, moving manufacturing to BCCs, and a refocus on secular growth opportunities.

Once Delphi emerged in 2009, the turnaround didn't stop there. As noted earlier, the Board and management helped drive a continuous improvement and lean culture that permeated the entire organization. This relentless focus on operational improvements and efficiencies became ingrained in the culture. By the end of 2014, O'Neal's last full year as CEO, EBITDA margins were over 15%, a 200 bps improvement since the IPO. Under new CEO Kevin Clark, EBITDA margins expanded a further 200 bps reaching nearly 17% by year-end 2017.

Buybacks & Dividends

As discussed, companies with long-standing buyback or dividend policies can be attractive investments. The continuation of an existing shareholder-friendly capital allocation strategy, however, does not constitute a catalyst *per se*. A true catalyst relies on the anticipation of a dynamic new stock repurchase program or dividend policy. A material change in capital allocation can serve as a watershed event, sending the stock price soaring. Large programs are particularly interesting, e.g., annual buybacks representing at least 5% of the float.

Activist investors often focus on capital returns as a value creation lever. A typical target has a large cash position and no apparent urgency to deploy that capital. Upon accumulating a meaningful stock position (often 5% or greater), the activist pushes management to repurchase shares or initiate a large one-time or regular dividend.

For Delphi, buybacks loomed as a potential catalyst due to its strong FCF profile, active Board, and lead shareholders. In January 2012, just two months after going public, the company announced a $300 million share repurchase program alongside its Q4'11 earnings release. This was quickly followed by a new $750 million authorization in September 2012 when the market cap was roughly $10 billion. The stock popped 3.5% on the news.

Then, at its investor day in February 2013, Delphi announced the initiation of a regular quarterly dividend. Per O'Neal: "*Our strong balance sheet and significant cash flow generation allow us to take this positive shareholder action today. The initiation of the cash dividend, along with our existing authorized share repurchase program, continue to reflect our confidence in the business and commitment to enhance shareholder value.*" Delphi's share price rose 9.4% over the next two days.

Refinancings

A refinancing can serve as a catalyst for revaluation. A common scenario involves an otherwise viable company that ran into trouble due to aggressive debt-financed expansion, a deep cyclical swing, or an overleveraged post-LBO capital structure. Shoring up the balance sheet serves as a catalyst for putting the company back on its feet. A distressed stock can turn into a big winner.

"Clean-up" refinancings take many forms. Perhaps the simplest involves obtaining a new or expanded credit line that provides liquidity. Or, a transaction that replaces high cost debt with lower cost debt, thereby boosting earnings and FCF. Similarly, a company may extend its maturities by negotiating with current creditors or refinancing existing debt with new, longer-dated paper. In more extreme cases, a debt-for-equity swap can lighten the debt load while providing lenders a share of the upside.

Post emergence from bankruptcy, Delphi had a clean balance sheet with plenty of liquidity. Annual interest expense was reduced from $750 million in 2007 to $125 million at its IPO. In late 2011, Delphi's bonds were yielding 6%, which demonstrated renewed confidence in the company from the debt markets.

Management Changes

Some investors look for situations where a new C-level executive can serve as a change agent. The company may be undermanaged, misguided, or simply in need of new blood. Clear underperformance vs. peers is a typical telltale sign.

Simply targeting companies where a new executive could serve as a catalyst is insufficient. The change must also be actionable. Perhaps the current CEO is on the verge of retirement. Or, the Board has signaled it is ready to make a change. An activist, of course, might make a new CEO or CFO the core of its agenda.

An external hire is more likely to be an agent for transformational change. This is particularly true for restructuring and turnaround situations, which require a specialized skill set. Often, the change agent comes from within the industry and has a stellar track record. Perhaps most interesting is when the management change is driven by the Board or activists with a clear agenda for unlocking value in the stock.

We already discussed Rod O'Neal's CEO tenure at Delphi starting in 2007. Several years later, in September 2014, investors had the opportunity to reassess Delphi with the passing of the baton to Kevin Clark. As noted earlier, the Board recruited Clark in 2010 due to his "high ceiling" potential. So, when the time came for O'Neal to retire, both the Board and investors had confidence in Clark as a worthy successor. Clark was expected to continue the focus on growth, operational excellence, and portfolio optimization.

As one research note summarized: "Changing of the guard – Legend passes mic to humble rock star … we are very confident in Delphi's management team, led by Kevin Clark, whose disciplined approach to capital allocation and vision were instrumental in creating today's Delphi." In this case, staying the course was a good thing.

Shareholder Activism

Activist investors don't buy a stock in anticipation of a catalyst and wait patiently. They take an "active" role in making the catalyst come to fruition. This is done by buying a sizable stake in the company and pressing for change. Prominent activist investors include Carl Icahn of Icahn Enterprises, Nelson Peltz of Trian Partners, Barry Rosenstein of Jana Partners, Paul Singer of Elliott Management, and Jeff Smith of Starboard Value.

While Delphi didn't have an activist *per se*, its investor base at the IPO included funds with proven turnaround track records and active investing approaches. Together, Silver Point, Elliott, Paulson, and Oaktree owned 45% of the shares. As large creditors in Delphi's bankruptcy, Silver

Point and Elliott gained ownership of Delphi stock through converting their debt holdings into equity. Their longstanding intimate knowledge of the company and key governance controls enabled them to play a leading role in shaping the New Delphi.

Silver Point and Elliott played a direct role in working with management to develop and execute the new strategic plan. On the governance front, they assembled a world-class Board in 2009 with backgrounds comprising automotive, technology, operations, capital markets, and corporate restructuring. The new Board was granted a private equity-style mandate to actively drive shareholder value. This meant intense Board engagement (far exceeding typical public company Board standards) with substantial pre-IPO equity participation for the new directors. The equity packages strongly aligned the directors' incentives with the value creation goals of shareholders.

Silver Point and Elliott also recruited operating specialists to assist management with key transition matters, cost improvements, and the rationalization of underperforming units. In a critical move, the new Board brought in Kevin Clark as CFO, whose background included both private equity and public company experience. As noted earlier, Clark eventually became Rod O'Neal's successor.

The lead shareholders and Board spearheaded Delphi's strategy around capital structure, allocation, and monetization. In April 2011, they orchestrated the $4.3

billion repurchase of General Motors' stock holdings in Delphi. Just a few months later, they took advantage of the summer/fall 2011 European credit crisis to repurchase an additional $180 million of stock. These actions reflected a culture that was fixated on equity value creation and positioning the company for a successful IPO. Going forward, the Delphi team became their own activists in the best sense of the word—tireless and forward-thinking stewards of shareholder capital.

From a technical point of view, the eventual sale of the core shareholders' stock provided yet another catalyst. While Silver Point and Elliott did not sell their shares in the IPO—a particularly bullish signal on their view of the long-term investment opportunity—over time, their shares would move into the hands of long-term institutional shareholders. As a general rule, a more permanent shareholder base helps remove an overhang and re-rate the stock higher. Buying into high quality businesses when concentrated owners exit has proven to be fruitful over time.

New Products & Customers

The successful introduction of major new products can translate into material new sales and earnings. A true game-changer leapfrogs the competition without cannibalizing sales of existing products. Upon announcement, the share price typically increases in anticipation of a new growth leg.

Large customer wins are similar to new product introductions. A material new contract represents additional sales and earnings not currently reflected in consensus estimates.

At Delphi, new product introductions related to Safe, Green and Connected were core to its strategy. By 2014, Delphi turned its attention to autonomous and self-driving vehicles, showcasing its latest product capabilities at the annual Consumer Electronics Show (CES) in Las Vegas. These included a 360-degree radar and imminent collision automatic braking platform. Then, in 2015, Delphi became the first company to launch a coast-to-coast, automated driving trial.

Delphi's focus on higher-tech, higher-growth, and higher-margin new products was not lost on investors. Expectations for enhanced profitability helped propel Delphi's P/E multiple to nearly triple that at its 2011 IPO by 2017. This was previously a level reserved for blue-chip industrial companies, not old-fashioned auto suppliers.

Regulatory

Meaningful changes in the regulatory environment create both opportunity and risk. For example, the announcement of a new transportation or infrastructure bill should serve as a catalyst for aggregates, cement, and ready-mix concrete companies. Similarly, new auto emission standards provide an opportunity for suppliers to drive higher margin content per vehicle.

On the risk side, be mindful of particularly sensitive industries such as energy, financial services, healthcare, and media & telecom. In energy, coal companies were decimated by EPA regulations regarding greenhouse gases. At the same time, this created an opportunity for clean energy to fill the void.

Antitrust regulatory considerations are relevant across all sectors. The Department of Justice (DOJ) must approve all business combinations above $90 million.[7] Therefore, any investment thesis or catalyst related to M&A activity needs to weigh the odds of receiving regulatory approval. The failed Comcast / Time Warner Cable (TWC) takeover in 2015 was a notable reminder.

Regulatory issues of a different kind thwarted Broadcom's (AVGO) $117 billion attempted takeover of Qualcomm (QCOM) in 2018—namely, national security. This deal was blocked on the basis of a recommendation by the Committee on Foreign Investment in the United States (CFIUS).

As previously noted, regulatory considerations were a key driver of Delphi's growth. In the company's core geographies, the implementation of increasingly tighter emissions and safety standards were catalysts. Each new standard was an opportunity for Delphi to introduce products and increase its content per vehicle. This also increased the company's stickiness factor with existing and new customers.

---

[7] As of February 20, 2019, subject to annual revisions.

How Catalysts Drove Delphi's Share Price

All told, meaningful catalysts provided clear guideposts for Delphi's ascent, driving a nearly five-fold increase from the 2011 IPO through the 2017 spin (see Exhibit 4.15). They comprised a combination of earnings beats, M&A, buybacks, and dividends, as well as well-received investor days and strong long-term guidance. A successful CEO transition and spin-off transaction also supported Delphi's incredible run.

EXHIBIT 4.15 DLPH Annotated Share Price and Volume History

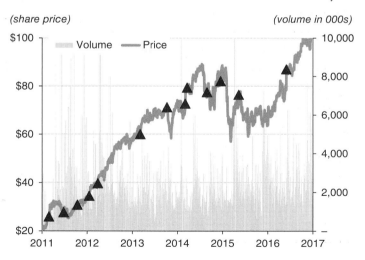

EXHIBIT 4.15 *continued*

▲ Date	Reaction	Event
1/26/12	+4.6%	Reported Q4'11 earnings and released 2012 guidance, both beating estimates
5/24/12	+7.6% (2 days)	Announced accretive acquisition of FCI's Motorized Vehicles Division (MVL)
9/13/12	+3.5%	Authorized $700 m share repurchase program
12/18/12	+10.3% (6 days)	Joined S&P 500, pre- and post-addition buying
2/26/13	+9.4% (2 days)	At investor day, initiated quarterly dividend (1.8% yield) and laid out long-term capital allocation plan
2/4/14	+8.1% (7 days)	Reported Q4'13 earnings (beating estimates), and confirming FY'14 guidance
9/9/14	-0.3%	Announced CEO Rod O'Neal's March 2015 retirement and succession by CFO Kevin Clark
2/4/15	+7.9% (4 days)	Reported Q4'14 earnings (beating estimates), strong buyback, and raised FY'15 guidance
2/19/15	-0.3%	Announced sale of Thermal Systems segment to MAHLE Behr GmbH & Co.
7/30/15	+7.7%	Announced acquisition of HellermannTyton
11/18/15	+8.4% (6 days)	Presented at Barclays automotive conference, outlined expectations for strong year
4/13/16	+6.6% (2 days)	Held investor day and laid out 2020 targets of 8% - 10% revenue CAGR and 18.5% EBITDA margins
5/3/17	+10.9%	Announced spin-off of Powertrain and creation of new connected/autonomous-focused company

Setting the Price Target

Now that you understand valuation and catalysts, how do you use this knowledge to pick a winning stock? Setting a price target (PT) is a critical next step. It is the culmination of your comprehensive due diligence and valuation work.

Your PT is the future price you expect a stock to reach if your investment thesis plays out. It is a core component of the ultimate investment decision, whether *buy*, *short*, *track*, or *pass*. Without it, you cannot properly quantify the upside potential and risk/reward trade-off.

The price target reflects the core market, intrinsic, and buyout valuation analysis already performed. This captures your financial projections and key catalysts. In many cases, the PT will be multiples-based, e.g., EV/EBITDA, P/E, P/FCF, or some combination thereof, with the closest comps serving as the main reference point.

In addition to your base case PT, you typically craft bull and bear cases. The risk/reward analysis is straightforward. Potential reward is measured by the percentage difference between the current share price and your base case PT. The bull case PT provides perspective on further upside potential. Your risk is reflected in the percentage difference between the current share price and your bear case PT.

Our PT analysis for Delphi is shown in Exhibit 4.16. We drove our base case PT off 2013E multiples for EV/EBITDA, P/E, and P/FCF. 2013E was chosen as the reference year for valuation as it allowed sufficient time for the auto recovery and Delphi's post-IPO strategy to play out. In other words, it reflected more "normalized performance."

Consistent with our thesis that Delphi should trade in line with the secular growers, we assumed multiple expansion in our base case. For the base EBITDA, EPS, and FCF/S, we relied upon the financial projections laid out in Step III (see Exhibit 3.11). These same projections were used to run our DCF in Exhibit 4.4, which yielded an implied share price of roughly $40. This was helpful as a sanity check.

For P/E, our base case 10x 2013E EPS of $4.36 led us to a PT of $43.64, a 98% premium to Delphi's IPO share price. For EV/EBITDA, we used 6x 2013E EBITDA of $2.4 billion to produce a PT of $40.57. And, 8% FCF yield based on 2013E FCF/S of $3.26 implied a PT of $40.79.

Our bull and bear cases incorporated tweaks to assumptions for both financial performance and multiples. For example, the Delphi bull case contemplated faster top line growth led by better U.S. and China volumes, higher margins, and larger buybacks. This resulted in 2013E EPS of $5.50. Multiplying this by an aspirational multiple of 12x suggested a PT of $66, or 200% upside.

Turning to our bear case, we assumed weakness in Europe, lower U.S. volumes, and lower growth for China, as well as higher expenses. This yielded 2013E EPS of $3.75. For multiples, we assumed they would stay flat to Delphi's IPO levels, i.e., in line with production-linked players. Applying a 5x P/E to a lower-growth, less-profitable version of Delphi yielded a PT of $18.75, or 15% downside.

EXHIBIT 4.16 Setting the Price Target

Delphi Price Target

($ in millions, except per share data)

	Base Case	Bull Case	Bear Case
Current Share Price	$22.00		
EV / EBITDA			
EBITDA (2013E)	$2,433	$2,676	$1,824
Target Multiple	6.0x	8.0x	3.5x
Enterprise Value	**$14,596**	**$21,407**	**$6,386**
Less: Total Debt	(2,173)	(2,173)	(2,173)
Less: Noncontrolling Interest	(462)	(462)	(462)
Plus: Cash	1,355	1,355	1,355
Equity Value	**$13,316**	**$20,127**	**$5,106**
Diluted Shares	328	328	328
Price Target	**$40.57**	**$61.32**	**$15.55**
Upside / (Downside) vs. Current Price	*84%*	*179%*	*(29%)*
Annualized Return	*36%*	*67%*	*(16%)*
P / E			
EPS (2013E)	$4.36	$5.50	$3.75
Target Multiple	10.0x	12.0x	5.0x
Price Target	**$43.64**	**$66.00**	**$18.75**
Upside / (Downside) vs. Current Price	*98%*	*200%*	*(15%)*
Annualized Return	*41%*	*73%*	*(8%)*
FCF Yield			
FCF / S (2013E)	$3.26	$4.08	$2.45
Target Yield	8%	5%	15%
Price Target	**$40.79**	**$81.58**	**$16.32**
Upside / (Downside) vs. Current Price	*85%*	*271%*	*(26%)*
Annualized Return	*36%*	*93%*	*(14%)*

Key Takeaways

- *Before valuing a company, you must first understand its business and underlying financials*

- *Your valuation work needs to determine whether the stock is attractive at today's price*

- *Even a stock that passes the business and financial test with flying colors may fail the valuation test*

- *Growth expectations are critical for valuation— investors tend to reward higher-growth companies with higher trading multiples*

- *While a company's valuation may appear attractive, tread carefully—more often than not the stock is cheap for a reason*

- *Look for catalysts that can meaningfully re-rate a stock through higher earnings power and multiple expansion*

- *Earnings compounders that deliver year-in and year-out are the traditional stock picker's bread and butter*

- *Ultimately, your valuation work must yield a defensible price target, which is the basis for the investment decision*

Chapter Five

Step V:
Investment Decision &
Portfolio Management

Time to pull the trigger?

You have identified a compelling investment idea, vetted it, and now must make a decision—*buy, short, track,* or *pass.* But, first let's take a step back and review how we got to this point.

In **Step I: Idea Generation,** we provided a framework for systematically sourcing potential investments. You learned how to screen for ideas based on valuation, financial metrics, and various corporate events, including M&A, spin-offs, and capital return. You also identified key macro and secular themes, and the most likely beneficiaries.

In **Step II: Identifying the Best Ideas**, you trimmed the list of potential investments on the basis of our idea review framework and investment write-up template, provided at **www.investinglikethepros.com**. You learned how to perform preliminary research focused on developing an investment thesis, evaluating a business, gauging management quality, assessing risks, and analyzing a company's financials and market valuation. Based on this initial work, you decided whether or not to continue exploring the opportunity.

In **Step III: Business & Financial Due Diligence**, you performed deep-dive fundamental research. You developed a true understanding of the business model, especially its key value drivers and risks. On the financial front, you examined the core financial statements to determine how the company makes, grows, and spends its money. In short, you formed a view on how the company will perform going forward.

In **Step IV: Valuation & Catalysts**, you determined what the company is worth. You also judged whether it is cheap or expensive, both on a standalone basis and vs. peers. Comps and DCF formed the core of this work with supplemental support from M&A-based valuation approaches, as appropriate. You also identified potential catalysts for driving a revaluation of the stock. This work culminated in setting a price target.

Now, in **Step V: Investment Decision & Portfolio Management**, it's time for the final verdict. In the event a *buy* or *short* decision is made, the work doesn't stop there. Going forward, the position must be constantly monitored for new developments that may change your initial thesis and PT, for better or worse.

If the stock is not compelling as a buy or short today, it can be placed in the *track* category. These stocks provide the seeds for future investments. They can be revisited later if a company's valuation or fundamentals change...or if a particular catalyst materializes. If you decide to *pass*, ideally that decision was made somewhere in the earlier steps.

Individual positions must also be managed within the context of the broader portfolio. Towards this end, we discuss fundamental portfolio construction and risk management techniques. Portfolio construction involves compiling a group of stocks that is tailored to your specific investment goals, strategy, and risk tolerance.

Correspondingly, risk management requires setting the proper risk/reward balance for your portfolio. Pay particular attention to position sizing, investment themes, sector concentration, geographic focus, and leverage levels. You also need to manage exposure to macro factors such as currencies, commodities, and interest rates. Key risk management tools include capping exposures, limiting losses, and profit taking, as well as hedging and stress testing.

Making the Investment Decision

Your due diligence and valuation work are complete. Now, you have a decision to make. This requires trust in your newly acquired skills and the courage to act. The proven ability to consistently make sound decisions over a long period of time defines a great investor.

Buy

You have followed our steps thus far and developed conviction in a given stock. This requires confidence in the business, financials, and valuation. It also means you believe the point of entry at today's share price is compelling. All of this fed into our assessment of Delphi at its IPO—namely, a clear BUY that offered secular growth at a cyclical price.

You do not want to fall into the trap of *good company, bad stock*. A great company can be a poor stock pick due to overpaying or mistiming. Microsoft is recognized as one of the most successful companies of all time, boasting a market cap of over $1.2 trillion at year-end 2019. Was it always a great stock pick though? As discussed in Chapter 1, after peaking at a $40 share price in late 1999, it took nearly 15 years for MSFT to break that ceiling.

As noted in Step IV, setting a PT prior to making the investment is a common best practice. It helps establish discipline and remove emotion from the decision-making process. Successful investors understand the parameters of their positions upfront and are prepared to exit as circumstances dictate.

Short

You have come to the conclusion that a stock is not a buy. But could it be a short? This decision requires the same level of diligence and conviction as a buy. Ironically, your search for compelling long opportunities may lead you to uncover ideas on the opposite end of the spectrum.

The decision to short a stock centers on the belief that it will decrease in value. The mechanics involve borrowing the shares (facilitated by a broker-dealer) and then selling them in the open market. Like anything borrowed, you ultimately have to pay it back. The short bet relies on being able to buy the shares back at a lower price in the future. Therefore, you profit from the spread between selling the shares at a given price today and buying them back at a lower price later.

During diligence, you may discover that the company or one of its peers is losing market share. Or, you may uncover a secular challenge to the business model, such as a change in pricing power or a low-cost emerging technology. You may even find a fundamentally inferior peer with unjustifiably high earnings estimates that is trading at a premium. Like Louis Pasteur, you may stumble upon an incredible discovery while looking for something else.

In general, short candidates are sourced from several common categories. These include external factors such as product substitution or obsolescence, structural pressures, shifting consumer preferences, cyclical peaks, and regulatory changes. They also include self-inflicted wounds, most notably accounting irregularities, mismanagement, overleveraged balance sheets, and misguided M&A. Common red flags include abrupt management turnover, unusually large insider selling, or a rapid succession of acquisitions.

Classic product obsolescence examples include the shift from print to digital media, e-commerce supplanting brick and mortar, and mobile devices displacing traditional cameras. Diligent short sellers were also rewarded by uncovering accounting malfeasance at Enron, SunEdison, Tyco, and WorldCom, among others.

Many investors use shorts on a tactical basis. This may be as part of a hedging strategy or selectively in the event a glaring short opportunity is discovered. There are very few pros, however, who have consistently made money with shorting as a primary strategy. Why? The market has a clear upward slope over time—since 1929, the S&P 500 has generated 11% annualized returns, including dividends reinvested. The short odds are also stacked against you due to ingrained institutional bias towards longs on the Street. Simply put, more actors stand to benefit when stocks are going up vs. down. You need to be highly skilled and selective to succeed given these circumstances.

Furthermore, your potential losses from a misguided short are unlimited. For a long position, if you buy a stock at $25 per share and the company goes bankrupt, your total potential loss is capped at $25. If you short a stock, however, there is theoretically no ceiling for share price upside. Your potential losses are uncapped.

Track

Some stocks may meet your business and financial criteria, but fail your valuation test. They are quality companies, but not currently cheap. Other stocks may be cheap but not quite attractive at the current time from a business or financial perspective. However, you see potential for them to improve and become long-term winners.

These ideas should be placed in the track category. As shown in Exhibit 5.1, our tracking sheet template lists relevant valuation multiples and other financial metrics for these stocks. Perhaps most importantly, there is a column for Price Target. This PT reflects your typical valuation work performed on the stock, as discussed in Step IV. When a stock on your tracking sheet trades at a meaningful discount to your PT (e.g., 25%+ within 12 months), you should be ready to revisit.

Ideally, you have been monitoring the company and keeping up-to-date on business and sector trends. In the event of a material share price decline, you need conviction that the drop is unwarranted and the original thesis remains intact. Alternatively, company prospects may improve such that you increase your PT. This may provide sufficient upside for you to reconsider the stock.

With every idea reviewed, you are building a database of potential core positions. In some cases, you may wind up tracking a stock for several years before it becomes compelling to own. Coming out of the depths of the Great Recession, some investors were able to buy high quality businesses they had been coveting for years at bargain basement prices. A time-tested value investing strategy centers on stockpiling quality ideas and then buying them opportunistically.

EXHIBIT 5.1 Tracking Sheet—Potential Ideas

Tracking Sheet

as of 3/1/2012

Company	Ticker	Current Share Price	Price Target	% Upside	Debt / EBITDA	EV / EBITDA '12E	'13E	'14E	P / E '12E	'13E	'14E	FCF Yield '12E	'13E	'14E
Amazon.com	AMZN	$180.04	$225.00	25%	0.7x	25.4x	18.1x	13.5x	64x	44x	33x	3.6%	4.8%	6.5%
Celanese	CE	$48.41	$55.00	14%	2.8x	9.1x	8.5x	8.1x	11x	10x	9x	4.5%	7.6%	8.2%
Charter Comm.	CHTR	$63.24	$85.00	34%	4.7x	7.4x	7.0x	6.6x	NM	NM	16x	7.4%	11.1%	15.8%
Danaher	DHR	$52.88	$55.00	4%	1.4x	10.7x	9.7x	8.8x	16x	14x	12x	7.4%	8.2%	8.8%
Google	GOOG	$622.40	$750.00	21%	0.2x	19.4x	16.4x	14.1x	15x	13x	11x	6.3%	7.4%	8.5%
Illinois Tool Works	ITW	$55.88	$60.00	7%	1.1x	8.3x	7.9x	7.5x	13x	12x	11x	7.4%	8.1%	8.8%
Mastercard	MA	$420.43	$500.00	19%	0.0x	11.6x	10.1x	8.8x	19x	17x	14x	5.1%	6.5%	7.5%
Priceline	PCLN	$637.32	$675.00	6%	0.3x	16.7x	13.0x	10.5x	24x	18x	16x	4.8%	5.8%	6.7%
Rockwood	ROC	$54.00	$67.50	25%	1.9x	6.6x	6.1x	5.8x	12x	10x	9x	7.1%	9.9%	11.3%
Sherwin-Williams	SHW	$103.56	$115.00	11%	0.9x	11.3x	10.6x	10.0x	18x	16x	15x	5.1%	6.1%	6.7%
Sirius XM	SIRI	$2.23	$3.00	35%	2.6x	14.7x	12.9x	12.1x	NM	28x	28x	4.6%	6.5%	8.7%
Time Warner Inc.	TWX	$37.46	$47.50	27%	2.9x	8.2x	7.7x	7.3x	11x	10x	8x	8.0%	10.5%	12.4%

Pass

The pass category is straightforward. This is a stock that you don't want anything to do with. It isn't compelling as a long, short, or future investment. Some passes you celebrate over time, others you regret. Regarding the latter, hopefully you can gain comfort with your rationale at the time, i.e., you followed the steps in our book and were methodical in your analysis. In the end, you simply made the decision that the stock wasn't for you. Discipline is a virtue—you don't want to force ideas into your portfolio.

Ideally, you made the decision to pass on a stock early in your investment process. Time spent on an eventual pass has a high opportunity cost. In the event the idea survived to this point, newly acquired knowledge can be applied to future investment opportunities. As you continue to research new sectors and companies, you continue to learn.

Monitor the Investment

The work doesn't stop once you initiate a position. You must follow your stocks closely and be prepared to adapt your thinking. New developments may change the initial thesis, sometimes at a moment's notice.

Monitoring your position involves constant reflection, analysis, and synthesis of company-specific and macro events that may impact the underlying business. *Your due diligence never stops.* You should always be reviewing and re-testing your thesis. Stay attuned to the risks you identified upfront.

The daily monitoring exercise centers on following company- and sector-specific news and research reports, as well as relevant economic data. On a quarterly basis, you dissect earnings releases and SEC filings, as well as accompanying investor presentations (if provided). Many pros also maintain a dialogue with investor relations (IR) or management. This extends to attending sector conferences where portfolio companies and their peers present.

Conversations with customers and suppliers also provide insight into industry dynamics and trends. This type of diligence helps you keep a healthy pulse on key value drivers and the competitive landscape. The same level of monitoring also applies to stocks on your tracking sheet so you can strike at the opportune moment.

We realize that if you're not a full-time investment professional some of the above work may prove challenging given time and resource constraints. But, if you're going to take stock investing seriously, you must be committed. We can provide the know-how but you must provide the can-do. We recommend that you carve out a block of time each day for portfolio work. At a minimum, you should read financial news on a daily basis and set up alerts for your focus stocks (e.g., Google Alerts).

Quarterly Earnings

Reviewing and processing quarterly earnings releases is a critical part of monitoring. Each quarter, U.S. public companies provide a full financial update and commentary on their prior three-month and year-to-date (YTD) periods, along with an accompanying 10-Q or 10-K and public conference calls.[1] Management also uses this forum to update investors on guidance/outlook, key strategic initiatives, and sector trends.

Your earnings work centers on comparing the company's quarterly and YTD results vs. prior year reporting periods, as well as vs. sell-side consensus and your own

---

[1] The time and access codes for these quarterly calls are provided on a company's corporate website. These calls are also typically webcasted, available for replay, and transcribed by various financial information services.

estimates. Quarterly sequential trends can also be informative for certain companies, particularly those that are less seasonal. Just as important, you should keep track of prior quarterly beats and misses, which may reveal meaningful trends.

Listen to the earnings calls and then review the transcripts as well as the sell-side research reports that follow. Pay attention to the substance and tone of management's comments, particularly on key performance drivers. Each stock has its own hot buttons with investors. For some, it may be top line growth, for others it's margins. Regardless, outlook and guidance trump all. Don't be surprised if a company beats on sales or EPS but trades down because management's guidance was uninspiring.

You should also spend some time reading through the 10-Q (or 10-K), especially the MD&A for color on the quarter. The footnotes to the financial statements are also informative. Pros typically seek a follow-up call with IR or management to clarify key areas of outperformance or underperformance. This call is also used to test financial model assumptions.

In Exhibits 5.2 and 5.3, we provide quarterly and annual earnings comparison templates for income statement and cash flow statement items. Your comparison sheet(s) may also include company- and sector-specific operating metrics, as well as segmented financials, if disclosed.

Our earnings templates below use Delphi's financial information for the fourth quarter ending 12/31/11, the company's first post-IPO earnings release. The annual template references Delphi's financial information for the full year ending 12/31/11.

In Q4'11, Delphi generated sales of $3.9 billion (+6.8% y/y), EBITDA of $530 million (+55% y/y), and EPS of $0.88 (+287% y/y), easily beating consensus estimates. In the same release, Delphi reported FY'11 sales of $16 billion (+16% y/y), EBITDA of $2.1 billion (+30% y/y), and EPS of $3.49 (+82% y/y). These dynamic growth rates reflected the rebound in Delphi's volumes off near-trough levels, improvements from cost-cutting initiatives, and operating leverage. Roughly two years after emerging from bankruptcy, the New Delphi's performance clearly reflected the company's striking transformational changes.

Key balance sheet metrics are also tracked. As shown in Exhibit 5.4, Delphi's leverage increased from 0.2x at year-end 2010 to 1x by year-end 2011. This was largely due to new debt raised to repurchase the $4.3 billion equity stake held by General Motors. On a net basis, Delphi's leverage was still only 0.3x given its large cash position. The company's 17.2x coverage ratio (12.1x on a capex-adjusted basis) was very healthy. Working capital intensity, as measured by NWC as a percentage of sales, increased slightly from 2.5% to 3.3%, which is not atypical for a fast-growing company. All in all, Delphi's balance sheet was in great shape.

EXHIBIT 5.2 Quarterly Earnings Comparison Template

($ in millions, except per share data)

Q4'11 Earnings Summary	Reported Q4'11	Reported Q4'10	$ Difference vs. Q4'10	% Difference vs. Q4'10	Beat / Miss	Consensus	My Estimates
Income Statement							
Revenue	$3,900	$3,652	$248	6.8%	Beat	$3,879	$3,898
Gross Margin	$679	$606	$73	12.0%	Beat	$581	$550
% margin	*17.4%*	*16.6%*	*0.8%*	*4.9%*	Beat	*15.0%*	*14.1%*
EBITDA	$530	$342	$188	55.0%	Beat	$419	$435
% margin	*13.6%*	*9.4%*	*4.2%*	*45.1%*	Beat	*10.8%*	*11.2%*
Net Income	$290	$75	$215	286.7%	Beat	$179	$217
% margin	*7.4%*	*2.1%*	*5.4%*	*262.1%*	Beat	*4.6%*	*5.6%*
Diluted Shares (1)	328	328	-	-	In Line	328	328
EPS	$0.88	$0.23	$0.65	286.7%	Beat	$0.54	$0.66
Cash Flow Statement							
Cash from Operations	$468	$287	$181	63.1%	Miss	$487	$456
Less: Capex	176	219	(43)	(19.6%)	Beat	187	175
% sales	*4.5%*	*6.0%*	*(1.5%)*	*(24.7%)*	Beat	*4.8%*	*4.5%*
Free Cash Flow	$292	$68	$224	NM	Miss	$301	$281
FCF /S	$0.89	$0.21	$0.68	NM	Miss	$0.92	$0.86
Capital Return							
Buybacks	$109	$0	$109	-	Miss	$136	$100
Dividends	93	2	91	NM	Beat	55	0
Total Capital Return	$202	$2	$200	NM	Beat	$175	$100
% of market cap	*2.9%*	*0.0%*				*2.5%*	*1.4%*

(1) Adjusted to reflect actual shares outstanding at the IPO for comparison purposes. Q4'10 reported EPS of $0.11.

EXHIBIT 5.3 Annual Earnings Comparison Template

($ in millions, except per share data)

FY'11 Earnings Summary

	Reported FY'11	Reported FY'10	$ Difference vs. FY'10	% Difference vs. FY'10	Beat / Miss	Consensus	My Estimates
Income Statement							
Revenue	$16,041	$13,817	$2,224	16.1%	Beat	$16,020	$16,039
Gross Margin	$2,655	$2,049	$606	29.6%	Beat	$2,633	$2,526
% margin	*16.6%*	*14.8%*	*1.7%*	*11.6%*	Beat	*16.4%*	*15.7%*
EBITDA	$2,119	$1,633	$486	29.8%	Beat	$2,011	$2,044
% margin	*13.2%*	*11.8%*	*1.4%*	*11.8%*	Beat	*12.6%*	*12.7%*
Net Income	$1,145	$631	$514	81.5%	Beat	$1,035	$1,072
% margin	*7.1%*	*4.6%*	*2.6%*	*56.3%*	Beat	*6.5%*	*6.7%*
Diluted Shares (1)	328	328	-	-	In Line	328	328
EPS	$3.49	$1.92	$1.57	81.5%	Beat	$3.15	$3.27
Cash Flow Statement							
Cash from Operations	$1,377	$1,142	$235	20.6%	Miss	$1,392	$1,356
Less: Capex	630	500	130	26.0%	Beat	641	629
% sales	*3.9%*	*3.6%*	*0.3%*	*8.5%*	Beat	*4.0%*	*3.9%*
Free Cash Flow	$747	$642	$105	16.4%	Miss	$752	$727
FCF / S	$2.28	$1.96	$0.32	16.4%	Miss	$2.29	$2.21
Capital Return							
Buybacks	$4,747	$0	$4,747	-	Miss	$4,763	$4,738
Dividends	93	27	66	244.4%	Beat	78	0
Total Capital Return	$4,840	$27	$4,813	NM	Beat	$4,818	$4,738
% of market cap	*68.5%*	*0.4%*				*59.6%*	*67.0%*

(1) Adjusted to reflect actual shares outstanding at the IPO for comparison purposes. 2011 and 2010 reported EPS of $2.72 and $0.92, respectively.

EXHIBIT 5.4 Balance Sheet Comparison Template

($ in millions)

FY'11 Balance Sheet Data

	Reported FY'11	Reported FY'10	$ Δ vs. FY'10	% Δ vs. FY'10
Capital Structure				
Financials				
EBITDA	$2,119	$1,633	$486	29.8%
Interest Expense	123	30	93	NM
Capex	630	500	130	26.0%
Debt Balances				
Cash	$1,372	$3,266	($1,894)	NM
Secured Debt	1,103	242	861	NM
Total Debt	2,103	289	1,814	NM
Net Debt	731	(2,977)	3,708	NM
Credit Statistics				
EBITDA / Int. Exp.	17.2x	54.4x	NM	
(EBITDA - Capex) / Int.	12.1x	37.8x	NM	
Secured Debt / EBITDA	0.5x	0.1x	0.4x	
Total Debt / EBITDA	1.0x	0.2x	0.8x	
Net Debt / EBITDA	0.3x	(1.8x)	2.2x	
Working Capital				
Current Assets				
Accounts Receivable	2,459	2,307	152	6.6%
Inventories	1,054	988	66	6.7%
Other CA	616	555	61	11.0%
Total Current Assets	**$4,129**	**$3,850**	**$279**	**7.2%**
Current Liabilities				
Accounts Payable	$2,397	$2,236	161	7.2%
Accrued Liabilities	$1,208	$1,265	(57)	(4.5%)
Total Current Liabilities	**$3,605**	**$3,501**	**$104**	**3.0%**
Net Working Capital	$524	$349	$175	50.1%
Working Capital Ratios				
NWC % of sales	*3.3%*	*2.5%*	*0.7%*	*29.3%*
Days Sales Outstanding (DSO)	56	61	(5)	(8.2%)
Days Inventory Held (DIH)	29	31	(2)	(6.2%)
Days Payable Outstanding (DPO)	65	69	(4)	(5.8%)

Portfolio Construction

So far, we have focused on finding winning stocks. Each individual position, however, needs to be considered within the context of the broader portfolio. A large position should reflect its relative ranking vs. your other stocks in terms of risk/reward profile. It should also reflect the timing for potential catalysts. In short, your highest conviction positions should comprise the largest portion of your portfolio. At the same time, be mindful of your overall investment strategy, goals, and risk tolerance.

Crafting a winning portfolio requires paying attention to exposure levels. Foremost among these is individual position sizing, which determines how much you can make (or lose) on a stock. You also need to be mindful of indirect exposures. These may include specific sectors, geographies, investment themes, currencies, commodities, interest rates, and leverage. Therefore, your initial portfolio construction work must ensure you're not taking directional bets on commodities or currencies, for example, without realizing it.

In some cases, you may be comfortable with concentrated exposure levels. Common examples include being overweight a specific stock, sector or geography. Similarly, if you believe cyclical stocks will outperform over the foreseeable future, you may be comfortable overweighting that investment theme.

Below, we discuss key portfolio construction considerations (see Exhibit 5.5).

EXHIBIT 5.5 Portfolio Construction Considerations

Portfolio Construction Considerations

- Investment Goals

- Risk Tolerance

- Position Sizing

- Sectors & Geographies

- Investment Themes

- Currencies

- Commodities

- Interest Rates

- Leverage Levels

Investment Goals

Setting clear investment goals at the onset is key for crafting a portfolio. First and foremost, let's focus on targeted returns. Is your goal to maximize absolute returns or beat a benchmark such as the S&P 500 or MSCI World?[2] Are you focused on achieving double-digit annualized returns, absolute risk-adjusted returns, income generation, or capital preservation? Regardless of the specific goals, your portfolio construction needs to be aligned.

These goals should also reflect your time horizon. Are you long-term focused, say three-to-five years or more? If so, you may have the staying power to weather potential dips along the way. Or, are you beholden to more frequent monthly or quarterly demands? In this case, you may sidestep highly volatile or illiquid stocks. For individual investors, personal liquidity requirements, retirement timeline, and return goals help dictate the time horizon. This becomes more complicated if you manage outside money and are subject to periodic reporting and redemptions.

---

[2] As of 2019, the MSCI World Index consisted of stocks from 23 developed market countries, representing ~85% of the market cap in each country.

Risk Tolerance

Risk tolerance is directly linked to your investment goals. An income-oriented or capital preservation strategy is inherently less risky than one aimed at maximizing returns.

You also have to be honest with yourself. A concentrated long portfolio, for example, can be subject to dramatic swings in either direction. Your temperament and conviction level is critical to seeing this type of strategy through. It also requires patient capital that will stay the course during periods of volatility. As British economist John Maynard Keynes famously stated, "the market can stay irrational longer than you can stay solvent."

Prudent portfolio construction also requires you to consider the volatility, or *beta*, of certain positions. A small-cap biotech stock, for example, invariably has a higher beta than a blue-chip consumer staples stock. So, if you're unable to stomach a potentially large drop (or *drawdown*) in a given position, you may want to minimize exposure to high-beta, volatile stocks. In the event one of your positions does experience a large drawdown, be sure to keep a cool head and not panic. Volatility may create opportunity.

Position Sizing

Approaches to position sizing can vary dramatically from investor to investor. Some view concentrated positions as essential to driving outsized returns. If you have a few high conviction ideas—so this line of thinking goes—it makes sense to back them. David Abrams of Abrams Capital and Seth Klarman of The Baupost Group come to mind as proponents of this philosophy. Others, however, believe in broader portfolio diversification.

Whether you're running a concentrated or diversified portfolio, your sizing approach should weigh the merits of each position relative to others. If you don't get the sizing right, you risk endangering your portfolio or missing valuable upside.

So, how do you size your stock picks? Should it be a 5%, 10%, or just a 1% "research" position? What is your conviction level with the particular stock at this point? Are there imminent catalysts that could drive the share price meaningfully higher? How does the risk/reward proposition compare to your other ideas? The PT work performed in Step IV is essential for force-ranking your positions and sizing accordingly. This enables you to construct a portfolio where the best ideas have the greatest weighting.

From a tactical standpoint, you may want to consider leaving dry powder, or excess uninvested capital, to size up opportunistically during market or company-specific hiccups. Maxing out your position early may mean missing out on the ability to buy future dips, especially during moments of market panic. Building a position over time also allows you to "scale into" your stock as you gain confidence in the thesis.

On the other hand, there may be situations where a max position is justified at the onset. This requires high conviction at an attractive entry price, or time sensitivity due to an imminent catalyst.

Sectors & Geographies

As with the sizing of individual positions, many investors have guidelines for max exposures to specific sectors and geographies. For example, you may limit your tech sector exposure to no more than 20% of capital. Or, you may cap your European exposure.

You also need to be mindful of the correlation between concentrated positions and the rest of your portfolio. If your largest position is an auto OEM, you may want to limit auto exposure in the rest of your portfolio. This way a sudden dip in the economy or auto cycle won't wipe out your returns. Don't get us wrong—if you have strong conviction in a particular sector or geography, being overweight is fine. Just be mindful of the risks and manage them accordingly.

There are constant reminders of the perils of over-concentration. Those heavily invested in energy heading into late 2014 and 2015 got hammered as oil prices fell precipitously. Other iconic examples include overexposure to internet stocks in the late 1990s, bank stocks in 2008, European stocks in 2011, specialty pharma in 2015, and retail in 2017.

Investment Themes

Investment themes refer to ideas centered on a specific corporate strategy or attribute. For example, your research may suggest that M&A platforms are likely to outperform given an attractive financing backdrop and market support. Other themes might be turnarounds, value stocks, growth stocks, earnings compounders, or cyclical plays at a perceived trough.

As with sector and geography, overconcentration in a given investment theme can be perilous. For an M&A strategy, a collapse in the debt markets could shut down those plays overnight. Similarly, for a strategy focused on cyclical troughs, your timing better be right.

Once certain themes become popular, they tend to attract a crowd. Fast money moves quickly, both in and out. Hence, despite the initial investment merits of these stocks, they are highly susceptible when circumstances change for the worse. It doesn't matter whether the problems are company-specific or market-based. Low conviction investors head for the exits. When things go wrong, you don't want to be the last one holding on.

Currencies

Currency exposure is a close cousin to geographic exposure. For portfolios with stocks that have significant international sales, currency fluctuations can meaningfully impact earnings and performance. For example, a steep drop in the Euro may dramatically affect a U.S.-domiciled stock with a large portion of its earnings in Europe. This is known as foreign currency translation risk.

A classic example occurred during the March 2014 to March 2015 period when the EUR/USD exchange rate dropped from 1.40 to 1.05, a 25% devaluation. As a result, a U.S.-domiciled company with 50% of its earnings from Europe would have seen a 12.5% decline in its reported USD financial results for that period based on currency alone.

At the individual company level, this risk must be identified and analyzed upfront. You need to understand how currency fluctuations can impact earnings and performance in various scenarios. This approach is then extended to the portfolio level where currency concentration can be hidden across multiple companies.

Commodities

"Commodity" stocks have higher cyclicality and volatility by their very nature. While the promise of super-cycles or "this time is different" thinking can prove seductive, you must give the commodity cycle due respect. A sudden shift in the price of oil, resin, copper, or steel—to name a few—can devastate an overexposed portfolio.

Dramatic commodity moves produce clear winners and losers. A sharp drop in oil prices hurts the producers' profits but helps the airline and trucking industries. Similarly, higher steel prices may help the mills but hurt manufacturers dependent on steel inputs for their products. This type of exposure can be mitigated through hedges in addition to capping position sizes.

Interest Rates

A portfolio's exposure to interest rate movements should also be managed. As witnessed in the post-Great Recession era, low interest rates can provide large tailwinds across the board. Consumers have incentives to spend vs. save on the margin. The same holds true for companies who have the ability to borrow at attractive rates to fund growth capex, acquisitions, and capital returns.

Conversely, tighter monetary policy characterized by rising interest rates can create headwinds, especially in the absence of a growing economy. High dividend-yielding stocks, as well as leveraged companies with substantial floating rate debt, are particularly vulnerable. Stories reliant on debt-funded growth, buybacks, or M&A are also affected. Portfolios overweight these stocks require heightened awareness and intelligence. You must be prepared to move decisively in the face of new information around potential rate movements.

Leverage Levels

Leverage is a double-edged sword. The proper balance can be a powerful tool for creating shareholder value. Cheap debt fuels organic growth, as well as accretive M&A and return of capital to shareholders.

During difficult times, however—whether macro-driven or company-specific—a heavy debt load can be damaging or even fatal. Many companies that entered the Great Recession with a highly-leveraged balance sheet went bankrupt. A combination of plummeting cash flows and the inability to refinance maturing debt proved insurmountable. Others survived but the shareholders' equity was seriously impaired and took years to recover, if ever.

Let's look at Charter Communications. By late 2008, after a multi-year debt-fueled acquisition binge, leverage reached nearly 10x. The associated high interest expense, coupled with sizable capex requirements, was crippling. Capex-adjusted coverage was under 1x, meaning CHTR didn't have enough cash to make interest payments. Furthermore, the company was unable to refinance maturing debt when the capital markets dried up during the Great Recession. In January 2009, Charter missed an interest payment and filed for bankruptcy.

After exiting bankruptcy in November 2009, Charter emerged with a significantly improved credit profile. Leverage was reduced to 5.5x and the company established a credible path to further deleverage. CHTR was a classic case of "*good company, bad balance sheet.*" It was also a victim of bad timing given the disastrous state of the capital markets in late 2008/early 2009. In a more constructive environment, the chances for refinancing would have been better.

You need to monitor leverage levels for both your individual stocks and overall portfolio. If the average leverage across your portfolio is 4x vs. the market at 2x, then a downturn would likely have a disproportionately negative impact on your performance.

Portfolio Summary

Portfolio construction goes hand in hand with portfolio risk management. You need to be diligent on the front end to protect yourself on the back end. In Exhibit 5.6, the upper tables show exposure by top 10 positions as well as their leverage. For example, Position #1, the largest, also has relatively high leverage at 2.8x. You can then extrapolate the same for positions #2 through #10.

On the upper right, the portfolio is segmented by market cap and liquidity. Over 40% of the portfolio is represented by stocks with market cap greater than $25 billion. Only 5% have market cap of less than $1 billion. In terms of liquidity, the entire portfolio can be sold down in 25 days or less. Of that group, 75% need only five days or fewer to exit.

By sector, the largest exposures are communications, discretionary, and technology. By geography, the U.S. represents 68% of the portfolio. The U.S. Dollar (USD), however, is slightly less at 65% given the U.S. companies' exposure to the EUR, GBP, and JPY, among others.

Taking stock of this illustrative portfolio in Exhibit 5.6, we made some key observations. First, it is relatively concentrated with the top 10 positions comprising 60% of holdings. As an offset, it is diversified by sector and also highly liquid. Second, while the overall portfolio is

moderately leveraged, certain positions tilt towards the high
end. There is also a fair amount of FX exposure. Having
flagged these potential portfolio hot spots, you may make
adjustments upfront or implement hedges for protection.

EXHIBIT 5.6 Portfolio Snapshot Template

Portfolio Summary					
Positions		**Leverage**		**Market Cap**	
Security	**%**	**Debt/EBITDA**	**High / Low**	**Size**	**%**
Position 1	10%	2.8x	High	> $25 bn	40%
Position 2	8%	4.7x	High	$10 - $25 bn	25%
Position 3	7%	1.4x	Low	$5 - $10 bn	20%
Position 4	6%	1.1x	Low	$1 - $ 5 bn	10%
Position 5	6%	0.0x	Low	< $1bn	5%
Position 6	6%	0.3x	Low	**Liquidity**	
Position 7	5%	1.9x	Low	**Days to Exit**	**%**
Position 8	5%	0.9x	Low	< 1 day	20%
Position 9	4%	2.6x	High	< 5 days	75%
Position 10	3%	2.9x	High	< 10 days	85%
Other	40%	2.0x	Low	< 25 days	100%
Total / Avg.	**100%**	**1.9x**	**Low**	> 25 days	-

Sectors		**Geographies**		**Currencies**	
Sector	**%**	**Geographies**	**%**	**Currencies**	**%**
Communications	20%	U.S.	68%	USD	65%
Discretionary	20%	Canada	2%	CAD	2%
Energy	-	Europe	18%	EUR	13%
Financials	5%	Asia Pacific	10%	GBP	8%
Health Care	2%	LatAm	2%	CHF	-
Industrials	15%	Australia	-	AUD	-
Materials	8%	Africa	-	CNY	-
Staples	10%	Middle East	-	JPY	5%
Technology	20%	Russia	-	HKD	5%
Utilities	-	Other	-	MXN	2%
Total	**100%**	**Total**	**100%**	**Total**	**100%**

Portfolio & Risk Management

As noted in Klarman's 2012 year-end letter: "We continuously worry about what can go wrong with each investment and the portfolio as a whole; avoiding and managing risk is a 24/7/365 obsession for us." Below we provide you with key tools to put this into practice.

Risk management must be performed at both the stock and portfolio levels. Just as each position must be monitored, so too must your entire collection of stocks. This involves a holistic assessment of the portfolio and the ability to quantify downside risks. Disciplined investors establish risk guidelines to optimize their portfolios and protect against losses.

Given the wide variety of funds and strategies, approaches to risk management vary accordingly. Multiple factors need to be considered, including target returns, risk appetite, fund size, investor base, capital stability, liquidity, and expected holding period.

The first step in effective risk management is to identify major portfolio hot spots. You can't measure and mitigate what you don't see or understand. As noted in Exhibit 5.6, these exposures may relate to a specific sector, geography, or currency. You also need to be prepared to quantify downside risk for various scenarios.

Ideally, key risks are flagged during your initial portfolio construction phase and a risk management strategy is mapped out concurrently. This means establishing an *early warning system* with clear thresholds for action. For example, if the investment thesis is based on an M&A strategy, you need to take particular notice if the financing markets dry up. Similarly, in a portfolio with heavy energy exposure, you need to be able to move quickly and decisively if your views on oil prices change.

Therefore, while successful investing requires a framework and discipline, it also requires flexibility. In a dynamic and ever-evolving market, it is critical to be adaptable and reassess your portfolio as new information comes to light. A stubborn allegiance to old views or bright lines may jeopardize performance.

If risk identification is the necessary first step towards effective risk management, then utilizing techniques for mitigating these risks is the second (see Exhibit 5.7).

EXHIBIT 5.7 Portfolio & Risk Management Tools

Portfolio & Risk Management Tools

- Exposure Caps

- Loss Limits

- Profit Taking

- Rebalancing

- Hedging

- Stress Testing

- Performance Evaluation

Exposure Caps

Perhaps the simplest method for managing risk is to set limits on the dollar or percentage amount for positions. This exposure may relate to single stocks or be aggregated by sector, geography, or investment theme. Some investors have hard and fast rules for sizing, e.g., a 10% cap for single stocks within the portfolio or 20% for specific sectors. Others are more flexible, allowing room to oversize best ideas while being cognizant of the risks.

According to a 2012 study by professors at Wharton and Booth,[3] nearly 45% of hedge funds had stated guidelines on the dollar value or percentage of assets that any one position can represent. The remaining 55% of funds had no restrictions. Clearly, many investors manage concentration risk through common sense and ongoing vigilance, as opposed to strict guidelines.

Loss Limits

In the event a stock pick is not working, there should be a mechanism in place to limit losses. This takes the form of share price downside thresholds that trigger revisiting your thesis to verify that nothing has changed—e.g., down 10%

---

[3]Cassar, G., Gerakos, J., 2012. *How do hedge funds manage portfolio risk?*

or 15%. Your downside PT work is particularly informative in this regard (see Step IV). It helps you avoid the trap of letting your original cost basis influence your go-forward decisions. The market doesn't care what you originally paid for a particular stock…

Stock investors have the luxury of participating in a liquid market where publicly-traded shares can be bought today and sold tomorrow. While this has obvious benefits, do not be lulled into a false sense of security. Drawdown guidelines in accordance with the aforementioned 10% or 15% dips can provide discipline for investors to reconfirm their thesis in a given stock. These guidelines may be tested by a major earnings miss, negative guidance revision, or other challenges.

If a position moves against you, your conviction level will be challenged. This is a difficult moment for any investor. A prized stock sells off on new data. You need to quickly assess whether this is serious or fleeting, and make a decision. The pressure is on. So-called experts are telling you that the stock is a loser. What do you do?

Regardless of the decision, you must avoid *confirmation bias* at all costs, i.e., cherry-picking information that favors your investment thesis. Loss limit guidelines help you avoid this bias and dispassionately exit if the thesis is "broken." These guidelines, combined with proper monitoring and risk assessment, were critical for evaluating Delphi post its late 2017 spin transaction. As with any major event, the investment thesis needed to be retested … and several factors had changed materially (as we discuss in the Post-Mortem). Fortunately, our system will have you prepared for these situations. If one of your positions isn't working, you must constantly ask yourself, "what am I missing?"

Of course, your reassessment may suggest that the stock is even more attractive given the new discount to your view of value. In this case, it might make sense to buy more. Real-time analysis and reassessment needs to be blended with strict adherence to guidelines.

Profit Taking

As the late investor Bernard Baruch wisely noted: *"Nobody ever lost money taking a profit."* Proper risk management often dictates taking profit opportunistically once your PT has been reached. This is particularly true when further upside appears limited.

Profit taking also applies if a stock skyrockets ahead of schedule. In a scenario where an investor purchases shares at $50 with a 3-year PT of $100, it may be wise to consider selling some stock if the share price reaches $75 within six months, for example. This also provides dry powder to add to the position if the price declines. Of course, a positive change to the thesis or upward earnings revisions may support holding on.

The PT serves as an important tool for guiding your approach to profit taking and helping protect us from ourselves. It is human nature for investors to fall in love with their best stocks, even more so when they are outperforming. Therefore, once the PT is reached, effective risk management forces you to actively reestablish conviction in further upside. This inevitably involves setting a new, higher PT based on updated information.

Rebalancing

Rebalancing your portfolio requires the same blend of common sense and guidelines that dictates overall risk management. You must always be ready to adjust your portfolio in line with new company and market data, as well as exposure caps, loss limits, and profit taking.

Let's examine an illustrative scenario where healthcare represents 20% of your overall portfolio. Over the next three years, your healthcare positions increase by 100% while the remaining portfolio is flat. As a result, your healthcare exposure is now 33%. Strict rebalancing would dictate that you revisit where to allocate the excess 13%. Of course, you may also decide that healthcare is the best place for that exposure and stay overweight.

In another scenario, you take profit in a large position and find yourself with dry powder. Your first move may be to allocate towards existing high conviction ideas. Alternatively, you could rebalance by investing in new stocks sourced from your tracking sheet or ongoing idea generation process.

Hedging

Hedging aims to mitigate risk by taking a position designed to offset potential losses from another investment. The actual hedge may take multiple forms, including offsetting stock positions, options, index futures, and various types of derivatives. Hedges can be used to offset idiosyncratic risks for individual stocks or the market as a whole.

We focus on offsetting stock positions and the use of options, such as calls and puts. It is important to note that it is not always necessary to hedge, and can be costly to do so. A truly diversified portfolio with a prudent risk management approach may be sufficient.

Pairing

A *pair trade* is a form of hedging where you go long one stock and short a similar one that you believe will underperform. The two stocks are typically within the same sector or serve the same end markets. For a given long, you seek an offsetting stock with inferior prospects. The goal is to realize profit as the long outperforms the short in rising and falling markets.

In 2016, a particularly successful pairing strategy in the media sector consisted of: 1) long Time Warner Inc. (TWX)[4]

---

[4] Not to be confused with Time Warner Cable.

and 2) short Viacom (VIAB). The thesis relied on TWX's ownership of must-have programming including HBO, CNN, and long-term sports rights, as well as Warner Brothers studio. The proliferation of online video was also creating more buyers for TWX's content. Meanwhile, VIAB was experiencing higher-than-average subscriber declines, lower ratings, and decreasing advertising revenues.

This pair trade proved successful with TWX outperforming and ultimately attracting a takeover offer from AT&T. As shown in Exhibit 5.8, $1 invested in TWX at year-end 2015 grew to $1.50 by the end of 2016. At the same time, $1 invested in VIAB decreased to $0.85, thereby generating significant *alpha*[5] on both sides of the trade. An investor who was long $1 of TWX and short $1 of VIAB would have made $0.65 on the combined trade.

EXHIBIT 5.8 $1 Invested in TWX vs. VIAB in 2016

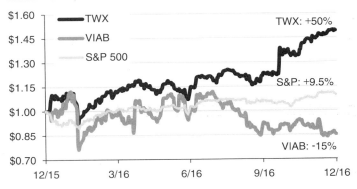

---

[5] Excess return over a market benchmark, such as the S&P 500.

Options

Options provide the contractual ability to buy or sell a stock at a set price by a predetermined date. A *call* provides the right to <u>buy</u> a stock at a set price (strike price) until a set expiration date. A *put* provides the right to <u>sell</u> at a set price by a set date. A typical options-based hedge consists of buying a put as protection against a potential long position decline.

For example, you own a stock that is trading at $50 but believe there is short-term downside risk. Let's say you buy a put for $1[6] with a $50 strike price. In the event the share price drops to $40, you can sell your shares at $50 and make a $9 profit ($50 strike price *minus* $40 *minus* $1 premium). If the stock instead stays above $50 through the expiration date, you only lose the $1 premium.

Options can also be used to express a long position without taking much risk. For example, let's assume a stock is trading at $50 and you believe it could rise to $60 over the next three months given a pending catalyst. However, if the catalyst doesn't materialize, there is risk the stock could drop to $40.

---

[6] The price of a call or put option ("premium") is typically determined in accordance with the Black-Scholes model. It depends on various inputs, most notably strike price, expiration date, and volatility of the underlying shares.

Instead of buying the shares at $50 and risking 20% downside, let's assume you can buy a 3-month call option with a strike price of $50 for a $1 premium. In this scenario, if the shares fall to $40, you simply lose the $1. Meanwhile, if the shares rally to $60, you have the option to buy the stock at $50 and make a $9 profit ($60 *minus* $50 strike price *minus* $1 premium).

Stress Testing

Stress testing is used to analyze hypothetical performance under various scenarios or "stresses." For example, you might test the effects of material USD, oil price, or interest rate movements on your holdings.

Ideally, during the portfolio construction phase, you identified key exposures for both individual stocks and the portfolio as a whole. For example, you should know what percentage of each company's profits are exposed to the energy sector. You can then sensitize how much a certain percentage move in oil prices could affect EPS and share price. We performed this exercise for Delphi's sales and EBITDA in Exhibit 3.7 with regards to auto production volumes, EUR, copper, and oil.

A simple approach for calculating share price impact would hold the P/E multiple flat (or more likely assume contraction) and multiply it by the pro forma EPS. This exercise is performed for all individual stocks and then aggregated at the portfolio level to determine downside scenarios.

Your stress testing should be guided by historical precedent. For the oil price example, you should test all the way down to (and potentially through) historical lows. You should also examine how a company's share price performed historically at given oil price thresholds. A portfolio stress test based on other factors (e.g., exchange rates or interest rates) should be governed by similar principles.

Performance Evaluation

You need to be able to measure your success. Pros typically benchmark their performance to an index, such as the S&P 500 or MSCI World. Others benchmark to a more specified or customized index in line with their investment strategy.

The ability to measure success requires a system that tracks performance at various intervals, e.g., daily, monthly, quarterly, annually. Investors with longer track records also benchmark performance accordingly, e.g., 3-year, 5-year, 10-year, and from inception (see Exhibit 5.9). Ultimately, your success will be judged by performance vs. your investment objectives and benchmarks.

As you review results vs. your benchmarks, seek to isolate key drivers of outperformance or underperformance. This helps you identify winning and losing strategies alike.

You can then rebalance your portfolio as appropriate with regards to individual stocks, sectors, or investment themes. For example, you may find that your turnaround situation picks have been consistent winners and overweight accordingly going forward. Or, perhaps you haven't performed as well in healthcare as technology, and decide to pivot in this respect.

Long-term success requires serious discipline and adherence to the basics, coupled with adaptability. Complacency is the enemy. Just because something worked for a quarter, year, or even longer, doesn't mean it will work forever.

In the event of sustained underperformance, you need to pause and take a step back. What isn't working and why? Revisit your overall portfolio strategy and risk management procedures. In short, go back to Step I and systematically retest and reconstruct the portfolio. Your analysis may actually find that the existing portfolio is solid with meaningful pent-up performance. In this case, perhaps the best strategy is to largely stay the course.

This same introspective approach applies to individual stocks. Upon exiting a position, look at how the stock's performance played out vs. your original thesis. This involves an honest assessment of what went wrong and what went right. Following this disciplined approach will lend towards success in future investments. Past mistakes can be avoided and winning formulas replicated.

EXHIBIT 5.9 Illustrative Historical Performance – Fund vs. S&P 500

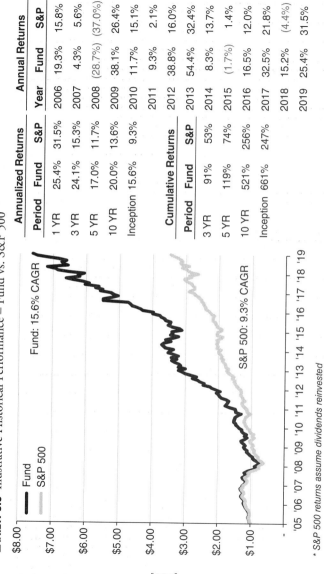

Annualized Returns

Period	Fund	S&P
1 YR	25.4%	31.5%
3 YR	24.1%	15.3%
5 YR	17.0%	11.7%
10 YR	20.0%	13.6%
Inception	15.6%	9.3%

Cumulative Returns

Period	Fund	S&P
3 YR	91%	53%
5 YR	119%	74%
10 YR	521%	256%
Inception	661%	247%

Annual Returns

Year	Fund	S&P
2006	19.3%	15.8%
2007	4.3%	5.6%
2008	(28.7%)	(37.0%)
2009	38.1%	26.4%
2010	11.7%	15.1%
2011	9.3%	2.1%
2012	38.8%	16.0%
2013	54.4%	32.4%
2014	8.3%	13.7%
2015	(1.7%)	1.4%
2016	16.5%	12.0%
2017	32.5%	21.8%
2018	15.2%	(4.4%)
2019	25.4%	31.5%

* S&P 500 returns assume dividends reinvested

Key Takeaways

- *Investment decisions require conviction—make sure you've done your homework*

- *Don't fall into the trap of good company, bad stock—the right entry price and timing are crucial*

- *Once you initiate a position, the due diligence never stops*

- *Position sizing should reflect a stock's relative risk/reward profile—your highest conviction stocks should have the highest weighting*

- *Portfolio construction needs to reflect your investment goals and risk tolerance*

- *Identify key exposures upfront and establish a risk management strategy accordingly*

- *Key risk management tools include exposure caps, profit taking, and rebalancing*

- *You must have the discipline to cut your losses in the event your thesis is "broken"*

- *Portfolio evaluation helps identify elements of your process/strategy that are working or need help*

Post-Mortem:
Delphi Automotive

Throughout the book, we used Delphi Automotive as a case study to illustrate how our 5-step process can be employed to source, due diligence, value, and ultimately manage stock positions. We took you back in time to the decision facing investors in November 2011 when Delphi was going public.

We then walked you through the tremendous success of the ensuing years culminating in the December 2017 spin-off. During this time period, investors were rewarded with a nearly five-fold return. By comparison, over the same period peer auto suppliers and the S&P 500 roughly doubled (see Exhibit PM.1).

EXHIBIT PM.1 Delphi Share Price vs. Auto Suppliers & S&P 500

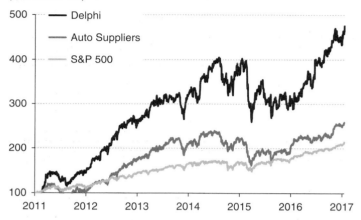

(indexed to 100)

The Delphi investment decision at IPO relied upon multiple drivers, perhaps best summed up by the opportunity to buy secular growth at a cyclical price. The global auto market recovery was in its early stages and Delphi had a powerful secular story centered on "Safe, Green and Connected," as well as a compelling growth opportunity in China. All of this was supported by a global best-cost footprint and a highly active Board and management team driven to create shareholder value. This created the opportunity for numerous catalysts, most notably earnings beats, share buybacks, and value-enhancing M&A.

As the share price performance clearly demonstrates, the seeds of the core thesis were firmly planted in the years leading up to December 2017 when Delphi Automotive split into two separate companies, Aptiv (APTV) and Delphi Technologies (DLPH). By that time, EPS had increased from approximately $3.25 at IPO to $6.75. The trailing P/E multiple also expanded from roughly 6.75x to 15.5x by the time of the spin (see Exhibit PM.2).

EXHIBIT PM.2 Delphi Valuation Progression from IPO to Spin

	@ IPO		@ Spin
EPS	$3.25	Organic growth Margin expansion Buybacks M&A	$6.75
	X		**X**
P/E	6.75x	Secular story Cyclical rebound Management Portfolio optimization	15.5x
	=		**=**
Share Price	$22		$103

At the same time, the spin transaction presented a natural capstone event for reassessing the investment thesis. First off, any spin merits *de novo* analysis given there are two new companies with distinct business models, strategies, and management teams. This was particularly relevant here given Aptiv's positioning as a premium auto technology pure play built around leading-edge businesses in active safety, infotainment, electrical architecture, and autonomous driving. Meanwhile, Delphi Technologies represented a pure play powertrain auto supplier whose fortunes were heavily tied primarily to global powertrain engine mix. These were two very different investment theses, indeed...

Furthermore, Delphi's meteoric rise from $22 to over $100 during the prior six years meant that profit taking, rebalancing, and other exit considerations were paramount. Per Exhibit PM.2, the P/E multiple was at a cyclical peak, representing a sizable premium to historical averages, and a solid premium to other auto parts suppliers. Add in a waning, late-stage auto cycle and the increasing drumbeat of trade tensions, and there were multiple reasons to revisit the overall investment thesis.

Post-Spin, 2019 and Beyond ...

Sector

In 2018, the global automotive market began to slow. Global auto production estimates were revised downward throughout the year due to a combination of weakening demand, U.S./China trade headwinds, and new European emissions testing standards. Commodities and currencies also hurt auto companies' financial performance. By year-end, auto production was down 1.0% y/y and consensus was calling for another down year in 2019.

Auto stocks were affected accordingly with the average supplier decreasing over 20% in 2018. Across the sector, sales and earnings estimates were guided down throughout the year and multiples contracted, creating a double whammy for share prices.

2019 proved to be more turbulent than initially expected as auto production estimates continued to trend downward, ultimately declining nearly 6% vs. 2018. The biggest culprits continued to be China weakness, trade headwinds, and negative revisions in Europe and North America, including the impact of the General Motors strike.

Overall, 2019 was largely a tale of the haves and have-nots for auto stocks. Those companies tied to strong secular opportunities outperformed and those deemed most susceptible to macro pressures continued to suffer.

Below, we discuss how the 2018 to 2019 period played out for both of the Delphi Automotive successor companies, Aptiv and Delphi Technologies.

Aptiv (ParentCo)

Following the spin transaction, Aptiv began 2018 on a high note. Its secular growth story at the nexus of auto connectivity, electrification, safety, and autonomous driving resonated with investors. Company performance was strong, standing out from other auto players grappling with the headwinds described above. Aptiv actually increased guidance through Q1'18 and Q2'18. By mid-June, the stock was up over 20%.

By the fall, however, negative sentiment around auto stocks intensified—even Aptiv's strong performance and compelling story couldn't fight the tape. In Q3'18, Aptiv delivered top line organic growth of 9% y/y, representing a 12% delta vs. production volumes down nearly 3%. However, management guided to a weaker Q4'18 driven by an anticipated slowdown in China vehicle production, albeit still with respectable 6% organic top line growth, roughly 8% to 9% above the market.

By year-end 2018, Aptiv's share price had fallen from its mid-June peak despite more than delivering on the original full-year 2018 guidance. On a fundamental level, the company's strong secular growth story remained intact, differentiating it from other auto suppliers ... and that story was ultimately rewarded in 2019.

Despite the broader macro auto headwinds, Aptiv established itself as a stock market darling in 2019. ESG (Environmental, Social, and Governance) and thematic investors dug in given Aptiv's now proven secular portfolio and better through-cycle performance, and Aptiv became one of the most widely held auto stocks. Towards the end of a choppy H1'19, the company held a well-received investor day where management reiterated its sustainable long-term growth and profit targets, as well as a compelling vision that extended through the middle of the next decade. Strong Q2'19 results lent further credibility to the story as a number of industrial and auto peers struggled.

Then, in September 2019, Aptiv announced the formation of a new joint venture with Hyundai centered on delivering its autonomous driving technology into production-ready vehicles. Aptiv's reputation for value-enhancing portfolio transactions, coupled with its Auto 2.0 positioning, further entrenched its status. By year-end, Aptiv was trading at $95 per share, not far off the pre-spin $103 share price for all of Delphi Automotive, outperforming all U.S. auto peers and more than making up for lost ground in Q4'18.

Delphi Technologies (SpinCo)

For Delphi Technologies, a.k.a., the legacy Powertrain Systems business, the macro headwinds were more pronounced. Negative mix factors related to the Delphi Technologies product portfolio and geographic exposure weighed on performance. Declines in diesel engine volumes, slowing production schedules due to new European emissions testing standards, and an abrupt slowdown in the local China market hurt Delphi Technologies disproportionately more than peers.

Compounding the above were some self-inflicted wounds related to execution, guidance, and communication to the Street. After initially increasing estimates post-Q1'18, management guided down the next two quarters. Unsurprisingly, this (mis)guidance exacerbated the negative reaction from investors.

Perhaps most damaging was the company's announcement on October 5, 2018, a true double jeopardy moment. In addition to disclosing that the CEO[1] had abruptly departed, Delphi Technologies dramatically lowered its 2018 full-year outlook. The stock tumbled nearly 13% that day alone.

---

[1] The Delphi Technologies CEO came along with the MVL acquisition and wasn't part of the pre-IPO management team.

Its formal Q3'18 earnings call on November 7, 2018 did little to appease investors as management gave a disappointing 2019 outlook. By year-end 2018, the stock had declined precipitously, a function of lower-than-expected earnings and significant multiple contraction.

As anticipated by the market, 2019 was largely a continuation of 2018 for Delphi Technologies. The company began the year by suspending its dividend, and investors questioned its ability to manage through unfavorable China OEM exposure and a choppy macro backdrop. Further, profitability was in question as Delphi Technologies sought to transition its legacy internal combustion engine products to a new generation of products, including those for electric vehicles.

However, towards year-end 2019, new leadership was focused on executing a "self-help" strategy based on a multi-pronged internal restructuring. The new plan was centered on operational rigor, including a right-sized engineering footprint, better launch readiness, and reduced SG&A, as well as double-digit growth in key product lines. Both the company and market viewed 2020 as an important transitional year to start delivering on these initiatives.

Then, in January 2020, competitor BorgWarner announced a deal to acquire the company for $3.3 billion, which translated into $17.39 per share. At deal announcement, this represented a 75%+ premium to Delphi Technologies' pre-deal share price. The combined company would have complementary products and a more complete portfolio in traditional internal combustion engine components, as well as enhanced electric vehicle component capabilities.

Per our discussion in Step V, the post-spin trajectories for both Aptiv and Delphi Technologies are important case studies for proper risk management. The December 2017 spin marked a clear inflection point for the original Delphi Automotive investment that necessitated a baseline reassessment. Rigorous position monitoring, thoughtful sizing, constant re-testing of the investment thesis, timely profit taking, and patience are critical for driving outsized investment returns.

Bibliography & Recommended Reading

Batnick, Michael. *Big Mistakes: The Best Investors and Their Worst Investments.* Hoboken, NJ: John Wiley & Sons, 2018.

Berntsen, Erik Serrano, and John Thompson. *A Guide to Starting Your Hedge Fund.* Hoboken, NJ: John Wiley & Sons, 2015.

Bruner, Robert F. *Applied Mergers and Acquisitions.* Hoboken, NJ: John Wiley & Sons, 2004.

Benello, Allen C., Michael van Biema, and Tobias E. Carlisle. *Concentrated Investing: Strategies of the World's Greatest Concentrated Value Investors.* Hoboken, NJ: John Wiley & Sons, 2016.

Damodaran, Aswath. *Investment Valuation: Tools and Techniques for Determining the Value of Any Asset.* 3rd ed. New York: John Wiley & Sons, 2012.

Dreman, David. *Contrarian Investment Strategies: The Psychological Edge.* New York, NY: Free Press/Simon & Schuster, 2012.

Klarman, Seth. *Margin of Safety: Risk-Averse Value Investing Strategies for the Thoughtful Investor.* New York, NY: HarperCollins, 1991.

Graham, Benjamin. *The Intelligent Investor: The Definitive Book on Value Investing.* Revised ed. New York, NY: HarperBusiness, 2006.

Graham, Benjamin, and Spencer B. Meredith. *The Interpretation of Financial Statements.* New York, NY: HarperBusiness, 1998.

Graham, Benjamin, and David L. Dodd. *Security Analysis*. 6th ed. New York, NY: McGraw-Hill Education, 2008.

Greenblatt, Joel. *The Little Book that Still Beats the Market*. Hoboken, NJ: John Wiley & Sons, 2010.

Greenblatt, Joel. *You Can Be a Stock Market Genius: Uncover the Secret Hiding Places of Stock Market Profits*. New York, NY: Fireside/Simon & Schuster, 1997.

Greenwald, Bruce C. N., Judd Kah, Paul D. Sonkin, and Michael van Biema. *Value Investing: From Graham to Buffett and Beyond*. Hoboken, NJ: John Wiley & Sons, 2001.

Koller, Tim, Richard Dobbs, and Bill Huyett. *Value: The Four Cornerstones of Corporate Finance*. Hoboken, NJ: John Wiley & Sons, 2010.

Koller, Tim, Marc Goedhart, and David Wessels. *Valuation: Measuring and Managing the Value of Companies*. 6th ed. Hoboken, NJ: John Wiley & Sons, 2015.

Lefèvre, Edwin. *Reminiscences of a Stock Operator*. Hoboken, NJ: John Wiley & Sons, 2007.

Leibowitz, Martin L., Simon Emrich, and Anthony Bova. *Modern Portfolio Management: Active Long/Short 130/30 Equity Strategies*. Hoboken, NJ: John Wiley & Sons, 2009.

Lynch, Peter, and John Rothchild. *Beating the Street*. New York, NY: Simon & Schuster, 1994.

Heins, John, and Whitney Tilson. *The Art of Value Investing: How the World's Best Investors Beat the Market*. Hoboken, NJ: John Wiley & Sons, 2013.

Marks, Howard. *The Most Important Thing Illuminated: Uncommon Sense for the Thoughtful Investor*. New York, NY: Columbia University Press, 2013.

Marks, Howard. *Mastering the Market Cycle: Getting the Odds on Your Side*. New York, NY: Houghton Mifflin Harcourt, 2018.

Mihaljevic, John. *The Manual of Ideas: The Proven Framework for Finding the Best Value Investments*. Hoboken, NJ: John Wiley & Sons, 2013.

Moyer, Stephen. *Distressed Debt Analysis: Strategies for Speculative Investors*. Plantation, FL: J. Ross Publishing, 2004.

Montier, James. *Value Investing: Tools and Techniques for Intelligent Investment*. Hoboken, NJ: John Wiley & Sons, 2009.

Nesvold, Peter H., Elizabeth Boomer Nesvold, and Alexandra Reed Lajoux. *Art of M&A Valuation and Modeling: A Guide to Corporate Valuation*. New York, NY: McGraw-Hill Education, 2015.

O'Shaughnessy, James P. *What Works on Wall Street: The Classic Guide to the Best-Performing Investment Strategies of All Time*. 4th ed. New York, NY: McGraw-Hill Education, 2011.

Porter, Michael E. *Competitive Advantage: Creating and Sustaining Superior Performance*. New York, NY: Free Press/Simon & Schuster, 1998.

Pratt, Shannon P., and Roger J. Grabowski. *Cost of Capital: Estimation and Applications*. 5th ed. Hoboken, NJ: John Wiley & Sons, 2014.

Reed, Stanley Foster, Alexandra Lajoux, and H. Peter Nesvold. *The Art of M&A: A Merger Acquisition Buyout Guide*. 4th ed. New York: McGraw-Hill, 2007.

Rittenhouse, L.J. *Investing Between the Lines: How to Make Smarter Decisions by Decoding CEO Communications*. New York, NY: McGraw-Hill, 2013.

Rosenbaum, Joshua, and Joshua Pearl. *Investment Banking: Valuation, LBOs, M&A, and IPOs*. 3rd ed. Hoboken, NJ: John Wiley & Sons, 2020.

Salter, Malcolm S., and Joshua N. Rosenbaum. *OAO Yukos Oil Company*. Boston: Harvard Business School Publishing, 2001.

Scaramucci, Anthony. *The Little Book of Hedge Funds: What You Need to Know About Hedge Funds but the Managers Won't Tell You*. Hoboken, NJ: John Wiley & Sons, 2012.

Schwager, Jack D. *Market Wizards: Interviews with Top Traders*. Hoboken, NJ: John Wiley & Sons, 2012.

Seides, Tim. *So You Want to Start a Hedge Fund: Lessons for Managers and Allocators*. Hoboken, NJ: John Wiley & Sons, 2016.

Shearn, Michael. *The Investment Checklist: The Art of In-Depth Research*. Hoboken, NJ: John Wiley & Sons, 2011.

Sonkin, Paul D., and Paul Johnson. *Pitch the Perfect Investment: The Essential Guide to Winning on Wall Street*. Hoboken, NJ: John Wiley & Sons, 2017.

Staley, Kathryn F. *The Art of Short Selling*. Hoboken, NJ: John Wiley & Sons, 2007.

Swensen, David F. *Pioneering Portfolio Management: An Unconventional Approach to Institutional Investment*. New York, NY: Free Press/Simon & Schuster, 2009.

Tracy, John A., and Tage Tracy. *How to Read a Financial Report: Wringing Vital Signs Out of the Numbers*. 8th ed. Hoboken, NJ: John Wiley & Sons, 2014.

Valentine, James. *Best Practices for Equity Research Analysts: Essentials for Buy-Side and Sell-Side Analysts*. New York, NY: McGraw-Hill, 2011.

Whitman, Martin J. *Value Investing: A Balanced Approach*. Hoboken, NJ: John Wiley & Sons, 2000.

Whitman, Martin J., and Fernando Diz. *Distress Investing: Principles and Technique*. Hoboken, NJ: John Wiley & Sons, 2009.

Whitman, Martin J., and Fernando Diz. *Modern Security Analysis: Understanding Wall Street Fundamentals*. Hoboken, NJ: John Wiley & Sons, 2013.

We hope you enjoyed reading our book as much as we enjoyed writing it. You now possess the essential building blocks for becoming a professional investor.

We wish you success in your investing endeavors.

—Josh & Josh

Email us at **josh@investinglikethepros.com**